BUNYAN'S
THE PILGRIM'S PROGRESS

Other Christian Guides to the Classics

Dickens's "Great Expectations"

Hawthorne's "The Scarlet Letter"

Homer's "The Odyssey"

Milton's "Paradise Lost"

Shakespeare's "Macbeth"

BUNYAN'S
THE PILGRIM'S PROGRESS

LELAND RYKEN

CROSSWAY
WHEATON, ILLINOIS

Bunyan's "The Pilgrim's Progress"
Copyright © 2014 by Leland Ryken
Published by Crossway
          1300 Crescent Street
          Wheaton, Illinois 60187

All rights reserved. No part of this publication may be reproduced, stored in a retrieval system, or transmitted in any form by any means, electronic, mechanical, photocopy, recording, or otherwise, without the prior permission of the publisher, except as provided for by USA copyright law.

Cover illustration: Howell Golson

Cover design: Simplicated Studio

First printing 2014

Printed in the United States of America

Unless otherwise indicated, Scripture quotations are from the ESV® Bible (*The Holy Bible, English Standard Version*®), copyright © 2001 by Crossway. 2011 Text Edition. Used by permission. All rights reserved.

Scripture quotations marked kjv are from the *King James Version* of the Bible.

Trade paperback ISBN: 978-1-4335-3463-8
ePub ISBN: 978-1-4335-3466-9
PDF ISBN: 978-1-4335-3464-5
Mobipocket ISBN: 978-1-4335-3465-2

Library of Congress Cataloging-in-Publication Data

Ryken, Leland.
    Bunyan's "The Pilgrim's Progress" / Leland Ryken.
      pages cm. -- (Christian Guides to the Classics)
    Includes bibliographical references.
    ISBN 978-1-4335-3463-8 (tp)
    1. Bunyan, John, 1628-1688. Pilgrim's progress. 2. Christianity and literature. I. Title.
PR3330.A9R95   2014
828'.407—dc23   2013032640

Crossway is a publishing ministry of Good News Publishers.

BP		24	23	22	21	20	19	18	17	16	15	14
15	14	13	12	11	10	9	8	7	6	5	4	3	2	1

Contents

The Nature and Function of Literature	7
Why the Classics Matter	8
How to Read a Story	9
Pilgrim's Progress: The Book at a Glance	12
The Author and His Faith	14
Literary Features	15
Bunyan's Allegorical Characters	16
Notes on Format	17

PILGRIM'S PROGRESS

Part 1

1	From the City of Destruction to the Wicket-Gate	18
2	Through the Wicket-Gate and in the Interpreter's House	22
3	The Perilous Journey from Interpreter's House to the House Beautiful	26
4	The House Beautiful	28
5	The Valley of Humiliation and the Shadow of Death	31
6	On the Road with Faithful	33
7	Vanity Fair	37
8	The Giant Despair	41
9	The Delectable Mountains and the Enchanted Ground	43
10	Entering the Celestial City	49

Part 2

1	Christiana Resolves to Flee the City of Destruction	53
2	The Journey from the City of Destruction to the Interpreter's House	56
3	Interpreter's House	59
4	Journey to the House Beautiful	61
5	Visit to the House Beautiful	63
6	Journey through the Valley of Humiliation	65
7	At the Inn of Gaius	69
8	Conclusion of the Perilous Journey	72
9	Saying Good-Bye to Life on Earth	75

Further Resources	78
Glossary of Literary Terms Used in This Book	79

The Nature and Function of Literature

We need to approach any piece of writing with the right expectations, based on the kind of writing that it is. The expectations that we should bring to any work of literature are the following.

The subject of literature. The subject of literature is human experience, rendered as concretely as possible. Literature should thus be contrasted to expository writing of the type we use to conduct the ordinary business of life. Literature does not aim to impart facts and information. It exists to make us share a series of experiences. Literature appeals to our image-making and image-perceiving capacity. A famous novelist said that his purpose was to make his readers *see*, by which he meant to see life.

The universality of literature. To take that one step further, the subject of literature is *universal* human experience—what is true for all people at all times in all places. This does not contradict the fact that literature is first of all filled with concrete particulars. The particulars of literature are a net whereby the author captures and expresses the universal. History and the daily news tell us what *happened*; literature tells us what *happens*. The task that this imposes on us is to recognize and name the familiar experiences that we vicariously live as we read a work of literature. The truth that literature imparts is truthfulness to life—knowledge in the form of seeing things accurately. As readers we not only look *at* the world of the text but *through* it to everyday life.

An interpretation of life. In addition to portraying human experiences, authors give us their interpretation of those experiences. There is a persuasive aspect to literature, as authors attempt to get us to share their views of life. These interpretations of life can be phrased as ideas or themes. An important part of assimilating imaginative literature is thus determining and evaluating an author's angle of vision and belief system.

The importance of literary form. A further aspect of literature arises from the fact that authors are artists. They write in distinctly literary genres such as narrative and poetry. Additionally, literary authors want us to share their love of technique and beauty, all the way from skill with words to an ability to structure a work carefully and artistically.

Summary. A work of imaginative literature aims to make us see life accurately, to get us to think about important ideas, and to enjoy an artistic performance.

Why the Classics Matter

This book belongs to a series of guides to the literary classics of Western literature. We live at a time when the concept of a literary classic is often misunderstood and when the classics themselves are often undervalued or even attacked. The very concept of a classic will rise in our estimation if we simply understand what it is.

What is a classic? To begin, the term *classic* implies the best in its class. The first hurdle that a classic needs to pass is excellence. Excellent according to whom? This brings us to a second part of our definition: classics have stood the test of time through the centuries. The human race itself determines what works rise to the status of classics. That needs to be qualified slightly: the classics are especially known and valued by people who have received a formal education, alerting us that the classics form an important part of the education that takes place within a culture.

This leads us to yet another aspect of classics: classics are known to us not only in themselves but also in terms of their interpretation and reinterpretation through the ages. We know a classic partly in terms of the attitudes and interpretations that have become attached to it through the centuries.

Why read the classics? The first good reason to read the classics is that they represent the best. The fact that they are difficult to read is a mark in their favor; within certain limits, of course, works of literature that demand a lot from us will always yield more than works that demand little of us. If we have a taste for what is excellent, we will automatically want some contact with classics. They offer more enjoyment, more understanding about human experience, and more richness of ideas and thought than lesser works (which we can also legitimately read). We finish reading or rereading a classic with a sense of having risen higher than we would otherwise have risen.

Additionally, to know the classics is to know the past, and with that knowledge comes a type of power and mastery. If we know the past, we are in some measure protected from the limitations that come when all we know is the contemporary. Finally, to know the classics is to be an educated person. Not to know them is, intellectually and culturally speaking, like walking around without an arm or leg.

Summary. Here are four definitions of a literary classic from literary experts; each one provides an angle on why the classics matter. (1) The best that has been thought and said (Matthew Arnold). (2) "A literary classic ranks with the best of its kind that have been produced" (*Harper Handbook to Literature*). (3) A classic "lays its images permanently on the mind [and] is entirely irreplaceable in the sense that no other book whatever comes anywhere near reminding you of it or being even a momentary substitute for it" (C. S. Lewis). (4) Classics are works to which "we return time and again in our minds, even if we do not reread them frequently, as touchstones by which we interpret the world around us" (Nina Baym).

How to Read a Story

Pilgrim's Progress, like the other classics discussed in this series, is a narrative or story. To read it with enjoyment and understanding, we need to know how stories work and why people write and read them.

Why do people tell and read stories? To tell a story is to (a) entertain and (b) make a statement. As for the entertainment value of stories, it is a fact that one of the most universal human impulses can be summed up in the four words *tell me a story*. The appeal of stories is universal, and all of us are incessant storytellers during the course of a typical day. As for *making a statement*, a novelist hit the nail on the head when he said that in order for storytellers to tell a story they must have some picture of the world and of what is right and wrong in that world.

The things that make up a story. All stories are comprised of three things that claim our attention—setting, character, and plot. A good story is a balance among these three. In one sense, storytellers tell us *about* these things, but in another sense, as fiction writer Flannery O'Connor put it, storytellers don't speak *about* plot, setting, and character but *with* them. *About what* does the storyteller tell us by means of these things? About life, human experience, and the ideas that the storyteller believes to be true.

World making as part of storytelling. To read a story is to enter a whole world of the imagination. Storytellers construct their narrative world carefully. World making is a central part of the storyteller's enterprise. On the one hand, this is part of what makes stories entertaining. We love to be transported from mundane reality to faraway places with strange-sounding names. But storytellers also intend their imagined worlds as accurate pictures of reality. In other words, it is an important part of the truth claims that they intend to make. Accordingly, we need to pay attention to the details of the world that a storyteller creates, viewing that world as a picture of what the author believes to exist.

The need to be discerning. The first demand that a story makes on us is surrender—surrender to the delights of being transported, of encountering experiences, characters, and settings, of considering the truth claims that an author makes by means of his or her story. But we must not be morally and intellectually passive in the face of what an author puts before us. We need to be true to our own convictions as we weigh the morality and truth claims of a story. A story's greatness does not guarantee that it tells the truth in every way.

THE
Pilgrim's Progress
FROM
THIS WORLD,
TO
That which is to come:

Delivered under the Similitude of a
DREAM
Wherein is Discovered,
The manner of his setting out,
His Dangerous Journey; And safe
Arrival at the Desired Countrey.

I have used Similitudes, Hof. 12. 10.

By *John Bunyan.*

Licensed and Entred according to Order.

LONDON,
Printed for *Nath. Ponder* at the *Peacock*
in the *Poultrey* near *Cornbil*, 1678.

Original title page

Pilgrim's Progress: The Book at a Glance

Author. John Bunyan (1628–1688)

Nationality. English

Date of first publication. Part 1, 1678, under the title *The Pilgrim's Progress: From This World to That Which Is to Come, Delivered Under the Similitude of a Dream*; part 2 published in 1684

Approximate number of pages. 250–300 or more (depending on size of pages and the presence or absence of illustrations and marginal notes)

Available editions. Multiple, including Barnes and Noble, Penguin Classics, Crossway (updated language and format, as well as original art), Oxford World Classics, Dover Thrift, Norton Critical Editions, Signet

Genres. Fictional narrative, allegorical narrative, dream vision, fantasy, realistic fiction, religious fiction, travel story, drama, adventure story, spiritual biography/autobiography, conversion narrative, drama, psychological narrative

Setting for the story. An imaginary realm that is too filled with symbols and archetypes to be simply identified with our known world, while at the same time having many of the qualities of our world

Main characters. Christian is the protagonist of part 1, and his wife, Christiana, is the protagonist of part 2. Once we move beyond those two, the number of characters explodes, but the following perhaps rise above the rest in prominence: Interpreter, who explains the truth of the Christian faith to Christian and his wife; Faithful, a sometime traveling companion of Christian who fled the City of Destruction shortly after Christian did; Hopeful, who becomes Christian's traveling companion on the last third of his pilgrimage (after Faithful is martyred); Great-heart, a soldier who serves as Christiana's guide and protector on her pilgrimage.

Plot summary. The story begins when the hero and narrator of the story resolves to flee his hometown called the City of Destruction. The main action for the remainder of part 1 is Christian's journey from the City of Destruction to the Celestial City. This is obviously the story of the salvation of the human soul. Every character and place that Christian encounters is either an aid or an obstacle in his progress toward Heaven and his growth in the Christian life. The main action is Christian's perseverance in the face of adversity and temptations to be diverted from his journey to Heaven. Part 2 is likewise a quest story in which Christiana and her children travel the same journey from the City of Destruction to the Celestial Gate. Christiana passes through most of the same places that her husband did and meets many of the same people, but there are enough new elements to make it more than simply a rerun of earlier action.

Structure and unity. The main structural element is named in the title and is a central genre in Christian literature as far back as the medieval writers Chaucer and Dante. It is the pilgrimage—a journey to a sacred place. *Pilgrim's Progress* is thus built around the quest motif, but of a specifically spiritual nature. The quest, in turn, plants this story solidly in the literary convention of the travel story and journey motif. Both parts of *Pilgrim's Progress* trace the progress of the protagonist from the lost state to the heavenly state. Part of the genius of the story is its tremendous momentum forward toward a goal. As in any quest story, in the two halves we follow the respective protagonists as they encounter a series of obstacles (chiefly places and persons) that seek to thwart the pilgrims' progress in the Christian life "from this world to that which is to come."

Cultural context. As a late seventeenth-century figure, Bunyan lived at the end of the original Puritan movement. He is a leading spokesman for that movement, and he drew his strength spiritually and culturally from the past. But the historical moment in which Bunyan lived is more complex than this personal allegiance to the past. Bunyan lived through the restoration of the monarchy in 1660. As a belated Puritan, Bunyan would have been completely out of step with the impious spirit of the new age, and in fact he was imprisoned for more than twelve years by the new regime for preaching without a license. We should also note that whereas the early Puritans such as John Milton were thoroughly classical as well as Christian in their intellectual allegiance, Bunyan's interests are more narrowly biblical and pietistic.

Tips for reading. (1) The most important prerequisite for enjoying this book as literature is the ability to abandon oneself to the travel motif and the adventure genre. At this level, the book is like Homer's *Odyssey* or Tolkien's Lord of the Rings—a continuous series of narrow escapes and threatening ordeals. (2) Equally, we need to relish the technique of allegory in which places and characters bear the names of abstract qualities. But the word *allegory* does not quite do justice to what is happening, so we need to add the concept of *symbolic reality*, which results when we enter a realm of the imagination in which the leading ingredient is a "forest" of symbols. (3) Putting the previous two points together, *Pilgrim's Progress* requires us to read at a physical level as the basis of everything else, but also to see that the two protagonists have undertaken a spiritual and psychological journey in addition to the physical journey. (4) The primacy of the spiritual governs everything that Bunyan does in the story and determines his storytelling techniques and choice of material.

The Author and His Faith

In his own day, John Bunyan was famous as both a preacher and a writer. He was of humble social standing and by his own estimate led a depraved life until his conversion in his early twenties. Viewed externally, Bunyan led a difficult life. He was poor from childhood. In his early teen years he followed his father's trade of itinerant tinker (mender of pots and pans). Bunyan's first wife died when he was thirty and left him to care for four children. Bunyan was intent on preaching outside of the authority of the Church of England and as a result found himself in and out of prison for much of his later life. Despite his chaotic external life, Bunyan was a prolific author. In fact, he published over thirty books, mainly doctrinal in nature. Bunyan also became something of a legend in his own time, partly because of his popularity as a preacher.

Several terms accurately describe Bunyan's religious beliefs and affiliations. As already noted, he belongs to the Puritan movement of the sixteenth and seventeenth centuries, and during his later teen years Bunyan was a member of Cromwell's Parliamentary Army. The word *nonconformist* is equally accurate and calls attention to the thing that landed Bunyan in prison after the restoration of the monarchy, namely, his refusal to subscribe ("conform") to the worship practices and ecclesiastical authority of the Church of England. Yet another word that was applied to a person of Bunyan's convictions was *dissenting* (or *dissenter*), meaning that Bunyan dissented from many of the beliefs and practices of the Church of England.

But the picture is more complex than these terms suggest. Soon after his conversion, Bunyan began to attend and then preach at the local Baptist church in his lifelong hometown of Bedford. At one point, local Quakers helped to secure his release from prison. If Bunyan were living today, he would be labeled a Reformed [Calvinistic] Baptist. But Bunyan disliked sectarian controversies, so we are on safest ground if we call him an evangelical Protestant Christian. He accepted the Bible as the authority for religious belief and as God's Word for daily spiritual sustenance. The doctrinal emphases that flowed from this commitment to the Bible were those of Puritanism. The starting premise is that all people are sinful by nature and are eternally damned until they are saved from their lost state. Personal conversion through faith in the atonement of Jesus is the starting point for the new life. The great priority in life is to be holy in one's conduct, and the goal of life is to enter Heaven in the life hereafter. This doctrinal framework provides the main thrust of the pilgrim's progress in both parts of Bunyan's masterpiece.

Literary Features

Pilgrim's Progress is the most paradoxical of literary masterpieces. When it stood alongside the King James Bible in pious Protestant households, it was read for spiritual edification as the Bible was. Literary sophistication was not on the radar screen of such readers, though that does not mean that they were not responding to the literary qualities of the book. The long history of people reading *Pilgrim's Progress* as a book of religious edification can easily mislead us, however. No other book in this series of guides to the literary classics incorporates more literary genres and modes than *Pilgrim's Progress* does.

The list of literary genres runs like this: fictional narrative; allegorical narrative; spiritual autobiography/biography; conversion story; dream vision (action presented as though it occurred in a dream); travel story; character sketch; parabolic writing (in which the literal details are obvious *examples* of some moral or spiritual reality); psychological narrative (a story about the inner life of the mind and emotions); hero story.

To this we can add the related category of literary modes that cut across genre lines: fantasy (unlifelike places such as the Delectable Mountains and characters with names such as Talkative); realism (some of it so rooted in Bunyan's local Bedfordshire that *Pilgrim's Progress* ranks as regional writing); symbolic reality (which occurs when the world that we enter as we read is made up primarily of events, characters, and objects that are symbols of something beyond themselves); drama (inasmuch as most of the book consists of dialogue and speeches); adventure story.

An additional set of literary terms comes into play when we analyze the prose style of *Pilgrim's Progress*. Relevant concepts include the following: realistic and colloquial prose; biblical prose, and more specifically King James style; descriptive/pictorial prose; dramatic prose; Puritan prose. Finally, as we read we encounter the great archetypes of life and literature on virtually every page. Some of these provide overall shape to the story, including the following: quest story, and more specifically a story of pilgrimage; the pilgrim; the journey through a landscape that is simultaneously physical, psychological (representative of states of mind), and moral/spiritual (as the allegorical names of the places continually remind us); the ordeal, and trial-by-ordeal; testing and temptation.

The bottom line is that the book is so obviously one of religious experience aiming at edification that only by an effort do we start to look upon it as a work of the literary imagination. When we make that transition, the floodgates suddenly open in a literary direction.

Bunyan's Allegorical Characters

Characters with allegorical names appear on nearly every page of *Pilgrim's Progress* and are obviously central to Bunyan's design for his story. These allegorical characters are created by taking an adjective (such as *faithful*) or noun (such as *evangelist*), capitalizing it (Faithful, Evangelist), and thereby making it what literary scholars call a "personified abstraction." Usually this technique produces thin characters, but Bunyan's allegorical characters defy that tendency and are triumphs of the imagination.

To begin, Bunyan's technique of characterization has a rich literary history behind it. Going all the way back to the Greek writer Theophrastus and running through Chaucer's portraits in the General Prologue to *The Canterbury Tales* is a literary genre known as "the character" (which in modern times we call the "character sketch" or "portrait"). Such character sketches tend almost automatically to produce what some eras have called "humor characters," meaning that the characters are unified or dominated by a single ruling trait (such as laziness) or role (such as merchant or wife). In turn, that technique often results in satiric portraits (portraits that expose human vice or folly).

Bunyan totally avoids giving us visual descriptions of his characters, but by some sort of magic the very names of his characters, accompanied by their actions, achieve the same effect as a portrait. The moment Bunyan calls a character "Pliable," we know who the character is: the person who is readily influenced by whatever outside force is before him at the moment and who quickly changes his mind and behavior when subject to the influence of that outside force. The allegorical name takes the place of a portrait, with the name itself being enough to create the character in an instant.

But that is only the beginning of the Bunyan magic. Bunyan's allegorical characters are multidimensional in the sense that nearly all of them represent three things simultaneously. (1) They are personality types—individuals with a propensity toward the trait named in the allegorical name (such as being talkative). (2) They are social types—people who have a certain effect as they mingle socially (for example, an overly talkative person quickly becomes a social pest). (3) They embody moral and/or spiritual qualities or effects. Most authors would be content with the first two layers of characterization, but because Bunyan is writing about the spiritual life, his originality in the enterprise is to push on to the third level and prompt us to think about how personality traits and social types can help or hinder a person in living a godly life.

We need to note also the immense range of Bunyan's characters, which cover nearly all the people we know. We do not readily think of Bunyan when we name the great creators of fictional characters, but he belongs on the list.

Notes on Format

The first issue to be resolved is what to call Bunyan's masterpiece. The main title of the book when it was first printed was *The Pilgrim's Progress*, but the title is usually shortened to *Pilgrim's Progress*, and that is the title used in this guide.

The second question is how to divide the text. As originally published, *Pilgrim's Progress* contains only two divisions—part 1 dealing with Christian, and Part 2 dealing with Christiana and her children. The book is often published that way, but just as often editors divide the material into units with titles. Depending on the edition, these units are called "stages" (of the pilgrimage) or "sections" (of the book). Sometimes the units are simply given titles, without further designation of stages or sections. Study guides necessarily divide the text into smaller units in addition to the two main parts of the book. In all cases, however, there is no uniform system of division. Instead, editors and commentators divide the material as seems best to them.

The author of this guide has divided the text into manageable units that will maintain uniformity with other classics that appear in this series. He has labeled the units "chapters" and has given each chapter a descriptive title based on the content of the unit.

Additionally, there is the matter of updated and abridged editions of *Pilgrim's Progress*, as well as simplified versions for children. Because this reader's guide marches through the text in sequence, it can be used with virtually any edition of *Pilgrim's Progress*. Quotations used in this guide preserve the archaic (King James) language of the original text, but the commentary is completely applicable to editions with modernized spelling. The commentary can also be used with abridged editions, on the understanding that the commentary may cover parts of *Pilgrim's Progress* not included in an abridgement.

In the quoted passages from the text of *Pilgrim's Progress*, not only has the original language been retained but also the original punctuation. Both of these make the book seem old rather than modern, and that is both accurate and part of the appeal of the story.

PART 1, CHAPTER 1
From the City of Destruction to the Wicket-Gate

Plot Summary

The opening line of *Pilgrim's Progress* is one of the most famous opening lines in all of literature: "As I walked through the wilderness of this world, I lighted on a certain place where was a den, and I laid me down in that place to sleep: and, as I slept, I dreamed a dream." The rest of the opening paragraph completes our introduction to the overall framework for the book—a framework known as the "dream vision." We also note that at first the fictional framework is narrated in the first person. This is largely dropped when the first-person narrator proceeds to tell the story of the pilgrim named Christian from the third-person point of view, but occasionally we return to the narrator with such formulas as *then I saw in my dream*.

The mainspring of the opening episode is that the protagonist is reading a book and is greatly disturbed by what he reads. In his distress, "a man named Evangelist" comes toward him, who points to a distant gate and urges Christian to proceed to it for help. Christian follows this advice and flees from his hometown called the City of Destruction. On the way, Christian meets characters named Obstinate and Pliable, who try to dissuade him from going forward with his journey, and a character named Help, who advises Christian on how to extricate himself from a life-threatening Slough of Despond (a bog) on the outskirts of town. Other characters whom Christian needs to fend off are named Mr. Worldly Wiseman and Mr.

It is impossible to overpraise the opening paragraph of *Pilgrim's Progress*. It wins us immediately with its first-person intimacy and its homespun realism (a den, sleep, dream, a man clothed with rags, a burden on the back). But we also experience the appeal and even thrill of allegory or symbolism, as we sense that these humble images of everyday life carry a level of meaning beyond themselves—a level of meaning that Bunyan as author entrusted to us to figure out.

An additional thing that we can note right from the start is that the language continuously reminds us of the Bible, and specifically the King James Version of the Bible. In addition to a general stylistic indebtedness to the Bible, there is a continuous chain of allusions to the Bible.

Legality. Evangelist comes to Christian's aid and counteracts the bad advice of that villainous pair, finally encouraging Christian one more time to proceed to the gate that will provide escape from destruction.

Commentary

The complexity of *Pilgrim's Progress*, despite its surface simplicity, is visited on us from the very start. This complexity lies in the fact that every physical detail, including characters and places, has a symbolic meaning that we need to decipher. Anything approaching fullness of interpretation is beyond the scope of this guide, and this is in every way a good thing because it activates readers of Bunyan's book and of this guide to complete the task of interpretation on their own or in small groups.

The autobiographical opening paragraph illustrates the technique of allegory or symbolism. The den where the narrator falls asleep is the jail in which Bunyan was imprisoned for preaching without a license. The dream that he dreams is the imagined story that he is about to tell. The "man clothed with rags," named Christian, is Everyman and Everywoman in the lost state. The book that makes Christian tremble is the Bible, with its doctrine of sin, and the burden on his back symbolizes the guilt and consciousness of sin.

With the allegorical wheels now set in motion, we witness the response of anyone who comes under conviction of sin. The lost state is symbolized by Christian's hometown, which is called the City of Destruction, referring to the destiny of Hell that lies ahead for anyone in an unregenerate or lost state. Evangelist is the preacher or religious

---

The original edition of *Pilgrim's Progress* printed a few Bible references in the margins of the text, and once the practice had been established, editions have often carried several hundred biblical references in the margins. Today, most editions, both scholarly and "popular," follow that practice.

Pilgrim's Progress is not (as is sometimes claimed) the first English novel. It has too many unrealistic elements, including the allegorical names, to be a novel. But there is a pervasive thread of native English realism in the book, and these touches are "novelistic." One of these real-life features comes early in the story when Christian falls into the Slough of Despond. This threatening bog comes right from the outskirts of Bunyan's hometown of Bedford, England. Bedford is close to the swampy area of England known as the Fens, and additionally almost all rural towns in Bunyan's day had mud holes and swamps, as there were no cement or asphalt roads.

instructor who informs Christian regarding what he must do to avoid the coming destruction that awaits him in his lost condition. The gate that becomes the first goal in this quest story represents the entrance into the experience of forgiveness of sins.

As is true in the early pages of any story that we read, we are feeling our way in the first chapter, gradually getting a picture of the ground rules that will govern the story as a whole. The entrance of the characters Obstinate and Pliable are our first hint that Christian's spiritual progress as he journeys onward will be impeded by characters who, if listened to, will sidetrack Christian from reaching the goal of his quest. Literary critics call these "blocking characters," and in *Pilgrim's Progress* they are invested with subtle religious and moral meanings that require us to ponder them. Obstinate stubbornly refuses to acknowledge any need to leave the City of Destruction, and Pliable, although he initially accompanies Christian out of the town, at once loses commitment to the venture when he slips into the Slough of Despond at the end of town. One constant ingredient in the plot is thus characters who give Christian bad advice or in other ways try to hinder his spiritual progress.

With the introduction of the Slough of Despond into the story we meet a second motif that will pervade the story: physical places that symbolize a moral or spiritual reality, either positive or negative. The Slough of Despond symbolizes despair brought on by conviction of sin. The village called Morality symbolizes the attempt to gain salvation by good behavior toward one's fellow humans. The house of Legality is an extension of that mind-set. The gate toward which Christian aspires

> "Do you see yonder wicket-gate?" Evangelist asks Christian. What is a wicket-gate? Nearly every reader of *Pilgrim's Progress* encounters this image for the first time while reading Bunyan's book. We are on safest ground if we simply accept this as a quaint British way of saying *gate*. A wicket-gate might open either into a building or a field; perhaps Bunyan envisions the latter, because when Christian passes through the gate, a character named Good-will points out the castle of Beelzebub "a little distance from this gate." What matters most is that for Bunyan there is a distinct point of division between being in the lost state and in the state of salvation. The biblical subtext for this detail in *Pilgrim's Progress* is the passage in the Sermon on the Mount where Jesus speaks of "the narrow gate" that "leads to life" (Matt. 7:13–14).

is also symbolic, but of something good, namely, entrance into salvation.

In addition to bad advisers and symbolic places, the story will continuously feature a succession of good characters who are positive influences on Christian in his quest to reach Heaven. Evangelist is the repository of theological truth, and in the early pages he is a never-failing fountain of spiritual insight for the searching protagonist of the story. In this particular episode, the instructive mission of Evangelist is to counsel Christian against heeding the attitudes pressed on him by such characters as Legality and to teach him the theological truth about how to be saved from sin. The character named Help plays a minor role compared to that of Evangelist, but he imparts good sense to Christian about using the steps that the King (also called Lawgiver) built for people to avoid being dragged down by the bog of despair over their lost state.

For Reflection or Discussion

Part of the genius of *Pilgrim's Progress* is that it requires readers to analyze the symbolic level of the story and in particular to figure out the nuances of the theological truth that is embodied in the narrative details. It is no wonder that this book has been a favorite in discussion groups. The main contours of reflection and discussion will be the same for all the units of the book: what does this or that detail symbolize, and what does it teach us about the Christian life? Of course the specific answers to those questions will be related to the phase in which Christian finds himself on his journey to the Celestial City. In this introductory unit of the story, we need to probe what the

Bunyan's allegorical characters, whose names consist of personified nouns and adjectives, might initially seem to be thin characters, but this proves to be untrue. The complexity emerges when we analyze the spiritual realities named by these character types, and additionally how these realities constitute threats to one's spiritual life. In this unit we can profitably ponder how Pliable, Mr. Worldly Wiseman, and Mr. Legality can divert one from spiritual progress.

story portrays about the lost state. Then we need to proceed to the experiential level: what forms have these realities taken in our own lives and those of our acquaintances?

PART 1, CHAPTER 2
Through the Wicket-Gate and in the Interpreter's House

Plot Summary

Having escaped the traps represented by such bad counselors as Mr. Worldly Wiseman and Mr. Legality, Christian is put back on the right path by Evangelist. "In process of time" Christian stands before the longed-for wicket-gate and knocks. A character named Good-will opens the gate, and Christian enters. Christian gives a brief traveler's account of his journey up to this point, and Good-will assures him that despite his litany of failures along the way, Christian is not cast out from salvation. In a brief instruction scene, Good-will points out a narrow way on which Christian must proceed.

The first stop will be at "the house of the Interpreter." Christian follows the instruction, and after repeated knockings at the door of the designated house is admitted by Interpreter. On the wall of a room in the house hangs the picture of "a very grave person" holding a book. This "authorized . . . guide" is never explicitly named, but we understand that he represents the Christian minister. The host and guest enter a parlor, where Interpreter "calls for a man to sweep." Dust flies everywhere. Then a maid sprinkles water to clear the air.

As the two move from one room to the next, they enter a room where they see "two lads" named Passion and Patience, and then a room where a fire burns against a wall that even water cannot quench. Behind the wall "a man with a vessel of oil in his hand" feeds the fire. Next Christian enters a beautiful palace with a heavily guarded door that he enters only after having been battered about. Once inside, Christian sees a man in an iron cage who despairs of ever leaving his miserable state. Entering a final room, Christian sees a man who trembles from fear after dreaming of the last judgment. The episode in Interpreter's house concludes with Christian resuming his journey.

Commentary

Because Bunyan was a man of minimal education, and because the style of the book is seemingly simple and straightforward, many people are lulled into thinking that *Pilgrim's Progress* will be an easy book to read. Any thought along these lines vanishes as we progress through chapter 2 of the story. Externally considered, chapter 2 is an interlude—a visit to a house between phases of journeying. Although the episode is relatively brief, it looks both backward and forward and is simultaneously an end to something and the beginning of something else. In short, it is a transition.

On the one hand, the passage through the wicket-gate is the goal of the first phase of the plot in which Christian progresses toward entry into a safe place. But the visit to the Interpreter's house ends by propelling Christian forward into the next phase of his journey.

> At many points, *Pilgrim's Progress* shows the Puritan beliefs and temperament of its author. The high regard for the minister and for preaching that we find in this chapter is entirely in keeping with Puritan values. A scholar once called the preacher the hero of the Puritan movement.

> The beating that Christian undergoes as he enters the palace is perplexing. While it may simply mean that the person pressing toward salvation meets persecution, it might also symbolize that a person must be divested of such things as "works righteousness" or reliance on the law (as opposed to grace). We should note that Bunyan teases us with the episode: he merely has Christian say, "I think verily I know the meaning of this," but does not disclose that meaning.

The conventions of allegorical narrative with a didactic ("teaching") purpose come into full view in this episode. The basic rule is that no matter how exciting the events are—so exciting that on a surface level we are reading an adventure story with surprises on nearly every page—nothing exists apart from an instructive purpose. One of the resulting conventions is that we need to settle down to reading many scenes of instruction in which someone imparts important information to the traveler. But the events do not happen only to the protagonist of the story; they happen to us, too, as the traveling companions of Christian. We, too, are dazzled by the endless succession of scenes and characters and bits of religious instruction that Christian encounters.

In reading *Pilgrim's Progress*, it is always important to analyze Bunyan's selectivity of details. The overall purpose of the book is to explain the nature of a Christian's experience, but why did Bunyan include the specific aspects of that experience that we find in his story? To call a house the "Interpreter's house" speaks volumes. The Puritans placed a very high priority on a person's grasp of Christian truth. That grasp requires us to interpret the Bible and theology accurately. It is no surprise that Bunyan highlights the importance of interpretation at this early phase of the pilgrim's progress in faith.

The commentary that appears in the margins for this chapter explains some of the specific details that appear in the visit to the house of the Interpreter. If we stand back from those details to get the big picture, something like the following emerges. Christian still bears the burden on his back (symbolic of sin and the lost state), and when he asks Mr. Good-will if the latter can help relieve him of the burden, he is told that he must bear it until he comes "to the place of deliverance." This means that the information and warnings that make up Christian's experience in the house of the Interpreter all have to do with preparation for salvation.

So what does Christian learn before he loses his burden? He learns that the preaching of the Word by ministers of the gospel will be a trustworthy guide. He learns the lesson of the dusty room—that the heart of those who are not yet in Christ is corrupt and that the law cannot cleanse the heart (something that only the gospel can achieve). He learns that attaining the life beyond requires patience (as embodied in the episode of Passion and Patience), that good works will not get him into God's kingdom, that paralyzing despair over the possibility of receiving God's grace and fear of final judgment will lose a person Heaven.

> The concluding moments in the Interpreter's House, involving "the iron cage of despair" and the man who fears the final judgment, have a long theological tradition behind them. According to this tradition, the worst of all sins is despair because it is a way of hardening oneself in refusal of repentance. To think oneself beyond the reach of God's grace is to doom oneself to Hell.

For Reflection or Discussion

One avenue toward appreciating Bunyan's narrative skill is to ponder his inventiveness in imagining scenes and characters that (a) captivate us at a literal level and (b) correlate to spiritual realities. This level of analysis relates to the story as a story. Then we can analyze what the successive units of action express about the spiritual life and in particular the spiritual aspects of life before conversion. This, in turn, can be pursued down two pathways—what the Bible says that correlates with Bunyan's portrayal and how we experience these realities in our own lives.

PART 1, CHAPTER 3

The Perilous Journey from Interpreter's House to the House Beautiful

Plot Summary

Upon setting out from the house of the Interpreter, Christian walks down a highway "fenced on either side with a wall, and that wall was called Salvation." Christian then quickly comes to a hill with a cross on the top. As he approaches it, the heavy burden that he has carried on his back falls off and tumbles in an open grave. Christian "gave three leaps for joy, and went on singing." To complete the transaction that has just occurred, three "Shining Ones" (angels, most likely) utter speeches that confirm the spiritual reality that Christian has experienced.

But this promising beginning for the next leg of the journey is quickly countered by a series of characters representing impediments to spiritual progress. The "first wave" of these characters whom Christian meets are Simple, Sloth, Presumption, Formalist, and Hypocrisy. To reinforce the danger represented by these tendencies in the spiritual life, Christian comes to the Hill Difficulty. Christian shows his earnestness in pursuing the Christian life by struggling to the top of the hill, and then new dangers meet him, again represented by characters who are personified qualities—Timorous and Mistrust.

Another nightmare experience is Christian's discovery that in his sleep he has lost the roll (piece of paper with a seal on it, the credential that will gain entry in Heaven) that one of the three Shin-

---

For Protestant Christians, the opening event at the cross is the most important thing that can happen to a person in this life. It consists of the forgiveness of sins in a once-for-all transaction. Conversion stories in the Bible and in the lives of Christians through the centuries provide a good context for understanding what happens to Christian at this moment in the story.

Bunyan's method in *Pilgrim's Progress* is to project spiritual realities onto physical images or pictures. The simplest and most numerous examples are the personified abstractions that make up the bulk of Bunyan's cast of characters. But other symbols of spiritual realities also abound. For example, sin is symbolized as a heavy burden and forgiveness as losing that burden. Most of Bunyan's great symbols are rooted in the Bible as well as the folk imagination. The indispensable source for exploring these symbols is a big reference book entitled *Dictionary of Biblical Imagery* (see Further Resources, p. 78). Articles in that book on sin and forgiveness provide

ing Ones had given him. So Christian retreads his steps, retrieves the roll, and hastens on. When Christian finally reaches the House Beautiful, a porter lets him in.

Commentary

The importance of this leg of the journey is disproportionate to the small amount of space given to it. Losing the burden of sin at the foot of the cross is one of the two most important events in the first half of *Pilgrim's Progress* (the other being Christian's entry into Heaven). Whereas the obstacles to spiritual progress that have befallen Christian up to this point have painted a picture of the life before conversion, the ones that happen now represent impediments in the spiritual progress of someone who has been converted to the Christian life.

At the level of travel story, the physical events in this episode are threats to someone who needs to reach a destination. Viewed thus, the events in this chapter resemble those that any traveler encounters—distracting characters, people who give bad advice, the physical ordeals of traveling, losing time by falling asleep, and needing to backtrack to find a lost passport. On this plane, this unit is one of Bunyan's nightmare passages.

But of course the second level at which the journey unfolds is the spiritual. We should view all the people whom Christian meets in this unit and the physical difficulties he undergoes as pictures of the temptations that befall Christians in their spiritual walk.

For Reflection or Discussion

At an allegorical level, Bunyan's intention is to give us a truthful picture of the obstacles to spiritual

---

helpful material for the biblical backdrop to the images that Bunyan chose to depict sin and forgiveness.

Formalist and Hypocrisy are characters rooted in Bunyan's Puritan experience. These two words (or variants such as *hypocrite*) were used by Puritans to denote people who went through the external forms of the Christian life such as church attendance and reciting of prayers without having received the new birth and without actually believing in Christ as Savior.

Many of the scenic details that Bunyan invented belong to the realm of literary archetypes—the recurrent master images of the literary imagination. These universal patterns recur in life as well as literature, but in literature they stand out silhouetted in such a way that we instantly recognize them. The Hill Difficulty is one of these images. Milton's Sonnet 9, written in praise of a virtuous young woman, begins with the hill of difficulty motif and makes good collateral reading for this episode in *Pilgrim's Progress*. Can you think of other examples?

growth that can occur in any Christian's life. With what details do you particularly resonate? How are the early days after Christian's conversion like the experiences of other people you have known? Why did Bunyan choose the specific spiritual vices that he did, as represented by their allegorical names? What real-life experiences or observations are embodied in Bunyan's personified vices?

PART 1, CHAPTER 4
The House Beautiful

Plot Summary

The previous chapter ended with Christian's awakening from his sleep, backtracking (and losing time) to find his lost roll, and then heading into the darkness with the threat of being attacked by animals seeking prey. He even hears two lions roaring at him. But then suddenly Christian sees a very stately palace before him, "the name of which was Beautiful," and he hastens to the door when the porter named Watchful shouts encouragement to him to proceed to the house.

After Christian's entry into the house, the porter passes him on to a virgin named Discretion. After that, the three virgins who live in the palace assume the major roles. They are named Piety, Prudence, and Charity. On the night of arrival, Christian's conversation with the three personified characters carries the action. Part of the conversation consists of Christian's recap of his travels, with the result that we experience some events in this story twice. A second ingredient is the questions that the three sisters ask Christian,

---

The last detail in the perilous journey immediately preceding Christian's arrival at the House Beautiful is two roaring lions that turn out to be chained (though in the darkness Christian does not see this). Interpretations of the lions by literary scholars suggest the allowable range of interpretation when we are dealing with an allegorical story. One editor is content with the general meaning of "the wicked people of the world." At the other end of the continuum is the view that the two lions represent the persecution of nonconformists [Puritans] by civil [governmental] and ecclesiastical [Church of England] authorities, a persecution that had been softened by the time Bunyan finished *Pilgrim's Progress* (hence the chained condition of the two lions).

either about his spiritual experience or his life story (including his family life).

The next morning is devoted to the instruction of Christian. The "records of the house" are read to inform Christian of the heroes of the faith. In the same vein, a visit to the armory of the house reveals the weapons with which heroes of the faith have achieved great things for God. The stay is prolonged when the sisters insist on showing Christian the Delectable Mountains in the distance. The visit reaches closure when Discretion, Piety, Charity, and Prudence accompany Christian away from the house to the edge of a valley.

Commentary

The rhythm of the story has now become fully established, and it is a universal pattern in travel stories from Homer's *Odyssey* and Spenser's *Faerie Queene* to C. S. Lewis's Narnia stories and Tolkien's Lord of the Rings. It consists of a predictable back-and-forth movement between journey along the path and temporary rest in a place, usually a house, palace, or castle. The rituals of arrival at the beginning and leave taking at the end encircle the stay at the residence. The main actions are (a) refreshment and renewal for the weary traveler and (b) instruction for the traveler but equally for the reader. The latter feature means that the author's didactic purpose is fully evident in these interspersed interludes. Bunyan hints at this when he includes the comment that the three sisters engage Christian in conversation before supper "for the best improvement of time."

One of the instructive aspects of the visit for both Christian and us as readers is the names of the characters: Discretion, Piety, Prudence, and

> Even in a heavily allegorical instruction scene such as the episode in the House Beautiful, Bunyan does not lose sight of the fact that he is telling a travel story. Accordingly, there is elaborate attention to the rituals of arrival, hospitality, meal, conversation, rest, and leave taking.

> It is always instructive to look up the Bible passages to which Bunyan explicitly or implicitly refers in a given detail of his story. These passages allow us to see Bunyan's imagination in the process of composition, and they also add depth of field to the details in his story.

Charity. We naturally get the point that these are essential virtues of the Christian life. Christian's recap of his journey likewise serves to underscore certain aspects of the Christian life, especially the pitfalls that threaten a pilgrim's progress. We learn still more about the Christian life through the information that we receive about the heroes of faith (the record book plus the armory). Finally, the glimpse of the Delectable Mountains in Immanuel's Land is a reminder to the pilgrim and to us of the goal of the Christian life.

There is a social dimension to the episode as well. We should note first the prominence of women in the scene. Their presence seems natural if we view the house as a picture of the local church and community of Christians. The names of the women are a picture of the specific type of refreshment to be found in Christian fellowship. Perhaps this Puritan note is reinforced by the two lions who roar but turn out to be chained: they may represent the authority of government and the meddlesomeness of the Church of England to nonconformist (Puritan) Christians like Bunyan himself.

> It is a convention of travel stories that when the traveler arrives at a place of rest, he narrates his story up to that point for the benefit of his hosts. Odysseus, for example, narrates the story of his adventures while visiting the Phaiaicans. However, in this instance there is something additional going on in the questions that the women at the House Beautiful ask Christian about his spiritual pilgrimage. The context includes the Puritan practices of spiritual self-examination (taking stock of one's spiritual state) and Christian conference (conversations with fellow Christians about spiritual matters).

For Reflection or Discussion

Whereas the journey episodes lend themselves to the double pleasure of external adventure coupled with symbolism about the spiritual life, the interspersed visits to places of rest (usually houses of some type) are more one-dimensional. The governing question for progressing through the visit to the House Beautiful is, What do we learn about the Christian life in the various details? Then we can explore Bunyan's skill as a writer in inventing the specific narrative details (as well as the range of such details) that serve as the vehicle for expressing insights into the nature of the Christian life. Additionally, are there any surprises for you as you ponder what aspects of the Christian life Bunyan chose for inclusion?

PART 1, CHAPTER 5
The Valley of Humiliation and the Shadow of Death

Plot Summary

When the journey resumes after the prolonged stay at the House Beautiful, Bunyan gives us a full-fledged, epic-style battle with a monster named Apollyon. The episode is worthy of the best single combats in fictional battles. The usual epic motifs are all there: the physical terror of the opponent (here a monster), the exchange of challenges and insults, a blow-by-blow account of physical combat, fluctuations in battle between the two combatants, yelling by the duelists, the final wounding of the villain, and battlefield thanks for victory.

But the battle with Apollyon is only one of two scenes of terror in this chapter. Bunyan identifies the next "sequel" as being one in which "Christian was worse put to it than in his fight with Apollyon." It is Christian's journey through a place called the Valley of the Shadow of Death. It is the archetypal evil place that even contains the mouth to hell. Christian passes through such terrors as flames of fire, dreadful noises, and a company of fiends coming toward him. He takes comfort in promises from the Bible, and at daybreak he finds himself

We need to understand right from the start that this chapter belongs to the genre of the horror story. At the surface level, Bunyan has built the story around what literary critics call "design for terror," meaning that he wants us imaginatively to relive the frightening things that Christian encounters. Beowulf's fights with three monsters in the Old English epic *Beowulf* make good collateral reading for this chapter.

The monster's name is Apollyon. This is the Greek word that means "destroyer," and Revelation 9:11 identifies the king of the bottomless pit as bearing that name. It is likely that Bunyan's terrifying monster is a composite of details that he found in his acquaintance with fictional chivalric romances and in various parts of the Bible, including the description of Leviathan in Job 41 and various monsters in the book of Revelation.

Bunyan's "The Pilgrim's Progress"

> When an author models an episode on a specific passage in the Bible, literary critics speak of the Bible functioning as a "subtext" and presence in the author's invented piece. There is no doubt that Psalm 23 functions as a subtext and presence in Bunyan's account of Christian's journey through the Valley of the Shadow of Death. Working out the correspondences is a good approach to this episode.

> Anyone familiar with Dante's story entitled *The Inferno* will find many resemblances between the fictional journey of Dante the pilgrim through Hell and Christian's journey through the Valley of the Shadow of Death. It is impossible that Bunyan had read Dante, but as already noted in this guide, the conventions of a literary genre such as the journey through the realm of spiritual evil are present quite apart from the influence of one writer on another. Familiarity with Dante's story can be useful as a guide to what we find in this chapter of Bunyan's story.

> If we are inclined to attach specific symbolic meanings to the ditch on one side of the narrow path

delivered "from all the dangers of his solitary way." At the end of the valley the pilgrim finds a pile of "blood, bones, ashes, and mangled bodies of men," as well as a cave "where two giants, Pope and Pagan, dwelt in old time." As Christian ascends out of the valley he meets a fellow traveler named Faithful.

Commentary

At a purely narrative level, the two episodes are among Bunyan's most inspired creations. They take their place among the best of epic and romance adventures and are triumphs of the literary genre known as "fantasy." Doubtless the book of Revelation was an influence on Bunyan's imagination when he composed this chapter. The journey through the Valley of the Shadow of Death is equally heightened, replete with such archetypal details as a place "as dark as pitch" and a narrow path with "a very deep ditch" on one side and "a very dangerous" bog or quagmire on the other. Adventures such as the two in this chapter require a childlike willingness to be terrified by monsters and dangers. C. S. Lewis's comment on Edmund Spenser's allegorical poem *The Faerie Queene* applies equally to *Pilgrim's Progress*: it requires a dual response, one childlike and the other sophisticated and able to figure out the allegorical meanings of the details.

On the allegorical level, then, we are given pictures of the power of evil in the form of what the Bible calls "principalities and powers." Compared to these giant threats, the more subtle obstacles to the Christian faith represented by people named Talkative and Timorous seem rather tame. The dangers through which Christian passes in this chapter are more than human.

For Reflection or Discussion

On the narrative level, the two episodes in this chapter are just asking us to remember parallel stories in classical epics and medieval romances, and the fictional stories of C. S. Lewis and Tolkien. The achievement of Bunyan will grow on us if we read a few parallel passages in other members of the same literary families. Then we need to draw correlations between the physical details of the adventures and what Bunyan is saying about the dangers to one's spiritual life and the means of overcoming those dangers.

> that leads to life and the quagmire (bog) on the other side, we are probably on safe ground in identifying the first as theological error and the second as carnal sin (immoral indulgence of physical appetites). The two giants named Pope and Pagan represent doctrinal heresy leading to damnation.

PART 1, CHAPTER 6
On the Road with Faithful

Plot Summary

Upon exiting the Valley of the Shadow of Death, Christian meets an old acquaintance named Faithful, who for us the readers is a new character. Faithful is from the same hometown as Christian was (the City of Destruction). As this chapter unfolds, it falls into two distinct halves.

The first half consists of a long conversation in which Faithful does most of the talking. First he fills in the details of what happened in the City of Destruction after Christian left on his pilgrimage. A leading incident is that Pliable was ridiculed in his hometown after he returned from his aborted trip to the Celestial City. Then Faithful recounts the details of his own journey from his departure from his hometown to the present moment. Highlights include his narrow escapes from a loose woman named Wanton and from a man called

> Bunyan is sometimes criticized for an allegedly individualistic conception of salvation in part 1 of *Pilgrim's Progress*, and the picture of Christian's abandonment of his family at the beginning of the story grates on some readers. But *Pilgrim's Progress* is an allegorical story in which the main story line is spiritual in nature. Bunyan's point is that every soul must be individually saved. To counter a possible misconception that he espouses a "lone wolf" brand of Christianity, Bunyan introduces traveling companions who represent fellow Christians who support the protagonist. Faithful is one of these companions, and he lends a communal aspect to the story of Christian's pilgrimage.

Adam the First at the foot of the Hill Difficulty. Like Christian before him, Faithful fell asleep and lost his roll. He of course traveled through the Valley of Humility and endured his own set of temptations (especially those posed by a character named Shame). The conversation ends with Christian briefly recounting his experience in the Valley of the Shadow of Death.

After this extended flashback, the second half of the chapter shifts the focus to the ongoing journey of Christian and Faithful. Their first encounter is with Talkative. Not knowing who he is, Faithful makes the mistake of inviting him to join Christian and him. To his credit, Faithful quickly infers that Talkative is someone who can talk on every religious topic that comes along and who substitutes talk for genuine spiritual experience. In private conversation with Faithful, Christian denounces Talkative at length, and an extended discussion ensues about the dangers of "talking" the Christian life but not living it. After this private "aside," Christian and Faithful resume the walk with Talkative, with whom they debate numerous religious points. Talkative eventually realizes that he is out of his depth with genuine spirituality, so he parts from Christian and Faithful.

Along with the two pilgrims, we feel a sense of relief when Evangelist makes an unexpected return to the story. Evangelist encourages the pilgrims to persevere in their journey to the Celestial City. He also forewarns them about dangers ahead.

Commentary

Up to this point in the story, the instruction scenes have primarily occurred in houses where Christian spends time between legs of his journey. In

> The character named Adam the First, encountered by Faithful at the foot of the Hill Difficulty, is a theologically laden symbol. It is based on New Testament comments about the first Adam in whom all fell, and the second Adam (Christ) through whom people are saved. Adam the First represents the futile attempt to win salvation through human works. Good collateral reading from the Bible includes Romans 5:12–21 and 1 Corinthians 15:21–22.

Bunyan's "The Pilgrim's Progress"

this chapter, long blocks of dialogue between the two travelers as they walk down the path are a blend of action and instruction.

In the introduction to his book *Reflections on the Psalms*, C. S. Lewis defines the essential principle of art as theme and variation—the same in the other. This is the working premise of the opening flashback in which Faithful narrates his adventures from the City of Destruction through the Valley of Humiliation. Faithful passed through some of the same places that Christian traversed, but he also bypassed some of those places. As Faithful tells his story, we gradually assemble a picture that partly resembles Christian's experiences but that in other ways is quite different from those experiences.

For example, Faithful managed to escape the Slough of Despond with ease, but on the path to the wicket-gate he was bothered by a woman named Wanton. Faithful passed the same lions (sleeping, this time) that had roared at Christian, but in contrast to Christian, Faithful did not stop at the House Beautiful, because he arrived there during daytime. The terrors that Faithful encountered in the Valley of Humiliation were quite different from the terrors that Christian endured there. The chief distraction was a character named Shame, who momentarily dragged Faithful down with shame over his spiritual failings. In summary, we are kept alert as we hear Faithful's account of his journey of the correspondence to Christian's journey and simultaneously of differences between the two.

Halfway through the chapter we shift gears. We leave past-tense accounts of the preceding journey behind and become absorbed in the present moment. The chief ingredient in this leg of the journey is provided by the allegorical figure of

---

Surprising as it may seem, the figure of Talkative may be Bunyan's self-portrait of what he was like before his conversion. Bunyan tells the story in his autobiographical *Grace Abounding to the Chief of Sinners*. On a day when Bunyan passed four women who were "talking about the things of God," Bunyan "drew near to hear what they said, for I was now a brisk talker . . . in the matters of religion; but I may say, I heard but understood not." As he heard the women talk "about a new birth, the work of God on their hearts," he realized how little he understood of the Christian life. This is exactly what we see in the figure of Talkative in this episode.

> Pilgrim's Progress is such a serious book that it is easy to overlook the latent comedy that sometimes comes to the surface. The comedy mainly resides in Bunyan's allegorical characters. Talkative is a comic type and a satiric portrait (satire as the ridicule of folly). He is a social pest whom we all know—the nonstop talker who mainly impresses himself but not others. Bunyan multiplies the humor by making Talkative the son of Say-well and someone who lives on Prating Row (equivalent of "Chattering Street"). Bunyan's originality consists of putting this comic social type into the context of Christian's spiritual pilgrimage and thereby prompting us to consider how superficial talking can be an impediment to the spiritual life.

Talkative. On one level, Talkative is a comic type held up to satiric ridicule and rebuke—a social pest whom we have all met. But as always in *Pilgrim's Progress*, the literal and social level of action embodies a spiritual level in addition. In our own jargon, Talkative talks the talk but does not walk the walk. He is very interested in religious matters and can talk about them indefinitely. But like the character Formalist earlier in the story, he is a stranger to the new life in Christ. All of his experience is head knowledge instead of heart knowledge. In relation to Christian and Faithful, he is a great distraction.

The reappearance of Evangelist at the end of the chapter is a breath of fresh air. He is a never-failing fountain of good sense about the Christian life. Bunyan reinserted him into the story at this point to remind the pilgrims (and us with them) of the goal of the journey. Accordingly, Evangelist paints a clear picture of the promised reward to those who endure to the end of the journey. He also states an ominous warning about an upcoming town called Vanity.

For Reflection or Discussion

Names are always important in *Pilgrim's Progress*, so analyzing them is a profitable exercise here and elsewhere. The names encompass both characters and places. The names themselves take on symbolic meanings and are comments on the Christian life; what are those meanings and comments? More specifically, what are the obstacles and diversions to Christians who seek the heavenly city? Overall, what do we learn about the Christian life in this chapter?

PART 1, CHAPTER 7
Vanity Fair

Plot Summary

The long conversation involving Christian, Faithful, and Talkative occurred on the path through what the story calls a "wilderness." We have already been alerted that the next stop will be a town called Vanity, at which a fair called Vanity Fair is held all year long. The bad feelings we have toward the place are immediately confirmed when Christian and Faithful arrive at the place.

Vanity Fair is a place of cheap and tawdry people, things, and activities. The pilgrims immediately attract the attention of the residents by their clothing, their speech, and their indifference to the wares for sale at the fair. That constitutes a problem for the travelers because the residents of the town and proprietors at the fair expect conformity to their own values and lifestyle. Christian and Faithful are first mocked, then beaten, and finally put into a cage. The two behave in such exemplary fashion that some of the townspeople begin to sympathize with them, and this in turn creates a division in the town of Vanity.

All of this eventuates in a formal trial of Christian and Faithful. The accusers are allegorical personifications, such as Envy and Superstition. The members of the Jury are equally villainous (Mr. No-good, Mr. Malice, Mr. Cruelty, and such like). The judge of this evil court is Lord Hate-good. Faithful is condemned and executed, and a divine chariot carries him up to the Celestial City. Providence, labeled as "he that overrules all things," intervenes in the situation of Chris-

---

The point has already been made that although *Pilgrim's Progress* belongs to the literary genre of fantasy (since most of the surface details are not things that we meet in the everyday world), the book nonetheless has some qualities that anticipate the rise of the novel a century later. This novelistic technique consists of literary realism or lifelikeness. It is well established that Vanity Fair is modeled on local annual fairs that Bunyan knew from real life.

As an extension of the realism of the event, we can also say that in the Vanity Fair episode Bunyan engages in social critique or social criticism. This means that he portrays the social life of his time from a critical standpoint. The literary vehicle for conducting such social critique is satire (the exposure of human vice or folly). Bunyan's choice of terminology for the object of attack is *vanity*, which in this context implies emptiness. Probably the source for this term is the biblical book of Ecclesiastes, with its famous statement "Vanity of vanities, all is vanity."

Bunyan's "The Pilgrim's Progress"

tian, with the result that he escapes from the town of Vanity.

A traveling companion named Hopeful immediately takes the place of the martyred Faithful, and the two set out on their path. In a pattern that is by now familiar to us, the pair meet a character name By-ends, from the town of Fair-speech, who boasts the acquaintance of such people as Lord Turn-about and Mr. Facing-both-ways. Mr. By-ends claims to be a religious person, but his religion is of the easy sort, so he falls behind Christian and Hopeful and meets up with such friends as Mr. Hold-the-world and Mr. Money-love. The story momentarily shifts the focus to this group and to their discussion of a religion of riches.

Two related events bring chapter 7 to a close. The money-loving group calls to Christian and Hopeful to stop, and then they make the case to the travelers that religion is meant to be profitable. Christian makes an extended rebuttal of that claim. Second, after Christian and Hopeful leave the worshipers of money behind, they come to "a delicate plain called Ease" and "a little Hill called Lucre." A gentleman named Demas invites the pair to come over to his silver mine. Christian refuses the offer, but as they turn back they see Mr. By-ends and his friends accept the offer of Demas and disappear into a pit. To clinch the point regarding the need to resist the love of riches, the travelers pass the pillar of salt into which Lot's wife was transformed when she looked back while fleeing from Sodom.

> The execution of Faithful doubtless comes as a great shock. Is the hostility of the world against Christians really that extreme? Throughout history to the present day, it has often been exactly that extreme. Bunyan's fictional character takes his place in a long line of martyrs for the faith. The literary genre into which this episode fits is called "martyrology" (the stories of martyrs). The most famous book of martyrology in the annals of English writing is one that Bunyan himself owned; it was written in the sixteenth century and is familiarly known as *Foxe's Book of Martyrs*.

Commentary

The episode of Vanity Fair became so famous in the cultural history of England and America that it has held the status of a proverb and familiar metaphor for the cheap and trivial. On the story level, Bunyan does two things to make the episode come alive in our imagination. First he draws upon his great descriptive ability to paint a verbal picture of a crowded local fair or concentration of street booths for selling trinkets and entertainment. He secondly creates a plot conflict of the utmost intensity as the evil crowd victimizes a pair of helpless travelers. This expands into a false trial with a stacked jury. Everything in the episode makes our blood boil in protest against what is happening.

As always in this story, the physical details embody profound spiritual meanings. A good interpretive framework by which to understand what happens spiritually in this episode is Jesus's statement recorded in John 16:33: "In the world you will have tribulation." Bunyan does a tremendous job of capturing the inherent bent of unbelievers to be intolerant of Christians and to find ways to persecute them because they do not share the values and lifestyle of an unbelieving world. In working out the implications of this hostility toward Christians, Bunyan in effect conducts his analysis largely by the names of the characters who afflict Christian and Faithful—names such as Envy and Carnal Delight and Live-loose. Naturally those values and behaviors are in conflict with those who live the Christian life.

The two halves of chapter 7 (as divided by the author of this guide) balance each other. The antagonists at Vanity Fair have no subtlety about them. They are figures of vice who are in open conflict with spiritual mindedness. Accordingly, Christian and Faithful endure persecution but are not tempted by anything. In a stroke of storytell-

> Mr. By-ends emerges as a leading character in the story in the second half of this chapter. The word *by-end* literally means "beside the main path," and by extension "something of secondary or incidental importance." This hardly takes us to the heart of Bunyan's character, something that we can ascertain when we observe the associations with which Bunyan surrounds him. Claiming to be religious, he lives at Fair-speech, moves among friends such as Mr. Anything, and is obsessed with money and upward social mobility. In short, he is a shallow person without strong convictions and someone who worships worldly success.

> Two items are continuously worthy of analysis with *Pilgrim's Progress*, including chapter 7. One is the allegorical names of characters as embodying insights into the Christian life and the things that undermine it. Another is the biblical references that are identified in the text and/or the margins. Tracing the biblical backdrop always gives us clues into what Bunyan intends in a given passage. The name Demas is merely a name until we look at 2 Timothy 4:10, where Paul writes, "Demas, in love with this present world, has deserted me." This is exactly what Demas represents in the story—love of the world rather than the gospel.

ing genius, Bunyan then creates a scene that is the exact opposite of the Vanity Fair episode.

The interaction between the travelers and the worshipers of wealth is a temptation scene par excellence. Here the danger is not external hostility but the allurement of worldly success. The allegorical antagonists are not bullies but qualities (such as Money-love and Save-all) that make life easy in the name of religion. Accordingly, what the conflict requires from Christian is the ability to provide convincing intellectual reasons against the claims that religious people can pursue wealth and success as their highest goals.

For Reflection or Discussion

There is no more modern or contemporary chapter in *Pilgrim's Progress* than this one. Our day specializes in the cheap and tawdry, and Vanity Fair in effect gives us an outline into which we can fit manifestations from our own culture. What links are suggested to you? Equally, the unwillingness of an unbelieving society to allow Christians to live their religious lives in peace is something that every Christian faces; what have been the examples of persecution and discrimination in your own life and observations? The temptations to a life of wealth and earthly success are also always at hand in the modern world; what forms have they taken for you? On a broader cultural scope, what are the current manifestations of the "prosperity gospel" that By-ends and his friends represent?

PART 1, CHAPTER 8
The Giant Despair

Plot Summary

As Christian and Hopeful pass the salt pillar of Lot's wife (a final reminder of the dangers of selling one's soul to riches), they come upon something entirely different, namely, a pleasant river with a paradisal garden on its bank. The river is called the River of God (also the River of the Water of Life). The path begins to swerve away from the river, but soon the pilgrims find themselves in a place called By-path Meadow. Its alluring pleasantness turns out to be a temptation that draws the pilgrims away from their quest. Walking is easy in the meadow, but it does not lead to the Celestial City, as the pilgrims discover when they catch up with Vain-confidence just in time to see him fall to his ruin.

Then follows another of Bunyan's nightmare passages. Rising waters prevent the pilgrims from returning to the path, so they seek shelter and sleep for the night. But their "little shelter" is near to "Doubting Castle, the owner whereof was Giant Despair." The giant accuses the pilgrims of trespassing and tosses them into "a very dark dungeon, nasty and stinking." On his wife's advice, the giant beats the pilgrims, leaving them "to mourn under their distress." Later he advises the pilgrims to commit suicide. The pilgrims are, indeed, in despair, but Hopeful calls them to the consolations of God's providence over them. There are daily visits from the Giant Despair, who abuses the pilgrims as his wife directs. But Christian remembers that he possesses a key called Promise, and by means of it the pair make their escape from the castle and

The alluring and life-giving river of life is a positive image with evocative biblical references behind it (Ps. 65:9; Ezek. 47:1–12; Rev. 22:1–2). However, Bunyan gives it an ironic twist. The technique he uses, beloved to storytellers, is known as "the false dawn motif." In this instance, the pilgrims' arrival at "the river of God" leads us to expect something completely good and fulfilling, but the brief paradisal interlude is only a momentary lull before a coming storm. The river of life and the paradise on its bank get only half a page, and then we are propelled into the next terrible adventure of the unfortunate pilgrims.

As always, names pack a big punch in Bunyan's story. Vain-confidence is a distinctly minor character, but we need to make something of his name and character. Vain-confidence is actually a projection of a trait that Christian exhibits in this chapter. It was Christian's idea to cross the stile into By-path Meadow, whereas Hopeful had urged them not to do so. Christian displayed confidence in his own judgment, and it was a false or "vain" confidence that got him into trouble.

return to the King's High-way. After recrossing the same stile that had gotten them into trouble at the beginning of the episode, Christian and Hopeful set up a sign warning pilgrims who would come after them not to step over the fence.

Commentary

The first item on the agenda with every episode in Bunyan's masterpiece is to relive the story on the literal level. In the course of just a few pages at the beginning of this chapter we encounter the archetypal river of life and earthly paradise, the difficult straight path (the proverbial "straight and narrow"), the beguiling meadow that diverts travelers from the right pathway, a giant, a castle, and a dungeon. All of these are stock ingredients of romance or fantasy stories, and they require a childlike willingness to be impressed and frightened by them. In the same vein, the repeated daily visits from the Giant Despair become a master suspense story, as we are led to wonder what violence will be visited on the pilgrims next and also whether they will escape alive.

Then we need to analyze the spiritual realities that Bunyan has embodied in these familiar narrative details. The centerpiece of the episode is the psychological and spiritual experience of despair. We have already noted in this guide that despair had a long history behind it by the time of Bunyan's day. In this tradition despair is considered the worst of sins because it paralyzes the will and leads people to view themselves as beyond the arm of God's ability to save. In effect it is a choice of eternal damnation, and nothing can be worse than that. These thoughts form the context for the prolonged, multi-day imprisonment in the dungeon of despair.

While part 2 of *Pilgrim's Progress* will do a lot with family relationships, part 1 is largely devoid of family matters. There are two main exceptions. The first is Christian's leaving his family behind when he escapes for his life from the City of Destruction (symbolic of how salvation is individual and is the most important thing in life). A second exception is the intriguing figure of Giant Despair's wife, named Diffidence. She is a mischief-making figure whose bad influence on her husband deserves analysis. As for her name, the word *diffidence* means "to be lacking in confidence." The giant's wife is certainly not lacking in confidence when she advises her husband regarding his two prisoners, so the best interpretation is to regard her as an extension of spiritual despair—the quality of lacking confidence in God's ability to save.

Within this as the general context, we can look more minutely at what Bunyan is embodying about the Christian life. For example, he gives us a detailed picture of how despair operates within a person's mind as an emotional phenomenon. Equally, we are led to trace the specific ways in which despair can keep a person away from pursuit of the godly way (called the King's High-way in the story). A third theme that we can trace is the resources that Christians (as represented by the two pilgrims) can summon to resist the destructive effects of despair in the spiritual life.

For Reflection or Discussion

The right procedure is to pursue the avenues laid down in the immediately preceding commentary. What narrative details make the episode come alive for you? What psychological realities do you vicariously experience as you read the episode? What can you see about how despair works in a person's spiritual life, and what are the trustworthy remedies to despair that Bunyan puts on the agenda of your awareness?

Chapter 8 is fed by the twin springs of literary fantasy or romance (with its unlifelike conventions of a giant and his castle and a symbolic river of life) and allegorical narrative (with its equally unlifelike conventions of names made from allegorical abstractions such as Despair, Vain-confidence, and Diffidence). But at every turn in this story everyday realism makes an appearance. The stile by which Christian and Hopeful cross into By-path Meadow and then out of it is a standard feature of the British landscape to this day. A stile is a ladder over a fence, whether a hedgerow or a stone wall.

PART 1, CHAPTER 9
The Delectable Mountains and the Enchanted Ground

Plot Summary

Anyone who is fond of long episodes will absolutely *love* chapter 9! It is filled with all that we have come to expect in Bunyan's adventure story: journeying, landscapes with spiritual meanings, allegorical characters who represent obstacles to spiritual progress, dialogue and speeches containing instruction in Christian doctrine, and the persevering champions of the faith named Christian and Hopeful.

The Delectable Mountains, first glimpsed by Christian from the roof of the House Beautiful, are another idealized pastoral world or earthly paradise. Four shepherds welcome the two travelers; they bear the allegorical names of Knowledge, Experience, Watchful, and Sincere. When the pilgrims are invited to the top of a hill called Error, they look down and see the mangled bodies of people who succumbed to theological error. From the top of Mount Caution the pilgrims see blind people stumbling about tombs; they are identified as victims of the Giant Despair. Then Christian and Hopeful look into the side of a hill and see fire and brimstone. From a hill called Clear the pilgrims can see the Celestial City. With these wonders behind them, and with certain warnings from the Shepherds ringing in their ears, the two pilgrims resume their journey.

First the pilgrims meet a character named Ignorance, who enters the pathway from a crooked lane leading out of the adjoining land of Conceit. Ignorance claims to know about an easy path to the Celestial City, but the two pilgrims dismiss the claim. Next Christian and Hopeful enter a dark alley where they see a man bound by seven devils; the man being thus led away is "one Turn-away, that dwelt in the town of Apostasy." This recalls to Christian a story of someone named Little-faith, whose tribulations are recounted at length. A leading moment in the misfortunes of Little-faith came when he was robbed by the rogues Faint-

---

Bunyan's place names are part of the magic of *Pilgrim's Progress*. They are often symbolic or allegorical in nature, belonging to a realm of fantasy or the imagination rather than the everyday world in which we live. They are almost always archetypes (recurrent in literature and life), awakening deep primitive feelings. The Delectable Mountains are the archetypal good place—an image of longing. The adjective *delectable* means "extremely beautiful and extraordinarily pleasant and delightful."

heart, Mistrust, and Guilt, with the result that he needed to beg for the remainder of his journey to the Celestial City. This, in turn, leads to a prolonged mini-sermon from Christian to Hopeful about how to withstand the obstacles to faith on the journey to Heaven.

The next main event in this chapter is the appearance of Flatterer, who claims to know the way to the Celestial City. Christian and Hopeful follow him and almost immediately find themselves caught in a net. They are rescued by "a Shining One" (either an angel or the Holy Spirit), who chastises them with a whip as punishment for their gullibility in following Flatterer. The two pilgrims then "go on their way."

They encounter Atheist, who shakes the composure of the pilgrims by announcing that he has been to the alleged place of the Celestial City, only to "find no more of it than I did the first day I set out." Momentarily startled, the pilgrims come to their spiritual senses and proceed. They enter a sleep-inducing territory called the Enchanted Ground, and in an effort "to prevent drowsiness in this place" they undertake "good discourse." A long conversation ensues in which Hopeful answers Christian's question of how Hopeful came "at first to look after the good of [his] soul." In effect we get Hopeful's spiritual autobiography.

The last episode in this chapter is the reappearance of Ignorance (who had been left behind early in the chapter). Hoping to instill religious truth in Ignorance, Christian and Hopeful undertake a catechism-like question and answer session. Ignorance is full of religious opinions but a slow learner in the truth of the Christian faith, and he eventually concludes that he "must stay a while behind." This

> It is no accident that the people who welcome the pilgrims to the Delectable Mountains are shepherds. They are the shepherds of the literary tradition known as "pastoral," an idealized green world. Pastoral is a picture of earthly life at its best. The characters who inhabit this beautiful rural landscape are always shepherds, figures of innocence. In the Bible, moreover, the shepherd of the pastoral tradition takes on the additional dimension of being a spiritual leader or minister.

leads Christian and Hopeful to analyze between them the reasons why people like Ignorance "know not that such convictions as tend to put them in fear are for their good" and therefore stifle them. At root, they conclude, is "the fear of the halter," that is, the dislike of anything that requires self-discipline and the curbing of one's natural desires. The chapter ends as Christian and Hopeful reach the far end of the Enchanted Ground.

Commentary

The first piece of useful advice is that we need to settle down to a long episode in which dialogue is the main ingredient. It has been apparent that some chapters of *Pilgrim's Progress* are packed with adventure on the path, and others are instructive units, usually set in places where pilgrims to the heavenly city temporarily stay. Chapter 9 combines those two formats. It is obviously a didactic chapter, or a "scene of instruction," but the instruction consists of long conversations as the pilgrims travel on the way, not at a house or castle. This chapter is low on adventure and high on talking.

This does not mean that the chapter is not entertaining. As always, the names of places and characters tease us into analysis of what they mean and how they are appropriate to the things that are thus named. An additional overlay is provided by the essential principle of *Pilgrim's Progress*, which we might call the primacy of the spiritual. No matter how inventive the fictional details of the story are, the narrative is ultimately governed by Bunyan's purpose of embodying information about the Christian life.

In turn, much of the instruction of *Pilgrim's Progress* consists of portrayal of obstacles to the

---

Sidebar: Literature makes its point by giving us positive examples to follow and negative examples to avoid. Little-faith teaches the importance of spiritual faith by negative example—by showing us what not to do. The Bible, as well as Christian theology based on the Bible, elevates faith to one of the most important virtues. Hebrews 11, which defines faith and celebrates the triumphs that it brings to followers of God, is good collateral reading for the story of Little-faith. A word search of *faith* in the Bible will also provide a good context for Bunyan's story of Little-faith.

spiritual life—beliefs and practices that can mislead a pilgrim and thwart his or her spiritual progress. A good strategy for working one's way through chapter 9 is to analyze the specific obstacles in the path of the Christian faith that Bunyan puts on the agenda for our consideration, and, further, to explore the exact ways in which each one can hamper one's spiritual life. The most obvious examples are doctrinal ignorance, flattery, weak faith, and atheism (the complete lack of faith).

One half of the instructive mission of chapter 9 is thus to give us further insight into what to avoid in the Christian life. The other half of the equation is Bunyan's analysis of the resources that the Christian can summon to counteract the dangers that Christians encounter. For starters, as we progress through chapter 9 we read about the benefits of true doctrine, of maintaining one's faith in the midst of temptation and persecution, of watchfulness in the spiritual life, and of godly conversation with believers.

Bunyan's allegorical characters are universal and timeless, and therefore always up-to-date in a reader's experience. The character of Ignorance, though, is unusually "modern" in his makeup. He wants to take a shortcut to Heaven instead of going through the wicket-gate and seeking the forgiveness of his sins at the cross. He is a religious person and is interested in religious matters. He can even say the right things, such as his comment that "I think I must believe in Christ for justification." But he believes that his heart is "a good one" and that he will enter Heaven on the basis of his good works. When asked how he is so sure about his religious convictions, Ignorance replies, "My heart tells me so." In short, he is the classic theological

---

The Enchanted Ground is another of Bunyan's great inventions. "Enchanted" in this case means "having magical powers." In fairy stories and fantasy stories, magic can be either good or bad. Here it is bad because it induces travelers to sleep when they should be trudging forward and keeping an eye out for dangers. The motif of places or drugs that rob people of their ability to be alert is as old as Homer's *Odyssey* and as modern as the fantasy stories of C. S. Lewis and J. R. R. Tolkien. Finding parallels in the stories with which you are familiar is a good exercise.

liberal, never more plentiful than in our own day. This is confirmed by the analysis of Christian and Hopeful after Ignorance decides to hang back instead of keeping up with the two pilgrims, as they put Ignorance into the category of people who lack "a change in their mind and will."

Bunyan was "a Puritan of Puritans," and the ideas and experiences that Bunyan chose to put into his masterpiece show a Puritan temperament at every turn. This is nowhere truer than in chapter 9 of *Pilgrim's Progress*. The importance of faith and knowledge or truth were pillars of the Puritan life and are embodied by negative example (that is, by their opposite) in the characters of Little-faith and Ignorance. When Christian and Hopeful decide to keep each other awake with conversation about their spiritual experiences, they are practicing what the Puritans called "Christian conference"—conversation among Christians on the spiritual life. Hopeful's autobiographical account of his conversion and his Christian walk are an example of Puritan's self-examination, and the stages of growth unfold according to the Puritan paradigm of salvation. The need to resist falling asleep on the Enchanted Ground illustrates the Puritan insistence that Christians must be *watchful* in their daily lives.

For Reflection or Discussion

A good approach to any story is to ponder a given episode and theorize about why the author included the chapter in the story and why he or she invented the specific details that we find in the chapter under consideration. Applying that framework to chapter 9, what do you think Bunyan intended with the chapter? In turn, it is always

---

Sidebar:

Good storytellers realize that they cannot keep going to the same well (figuratively speaking), so they find ways to vary their presentation. One time-honored technique is known as "the story within a story," and it makes an appearance here when the narrator of *Pilgrim's Progress*, instead of himself telling the story of Little-faith, allows Christian to tell the story to another internal character in Bunyan's story (Hopeful). A variation on that technique is known as the "flashback," illustrated by Hopeful's autobiographical account of his conversion and spiritual progress.

Bunyan's purpose in *Pilgrim's Progress* to illuminate the Christian life. Since this chapter is too expansive to analyze all at once, a good exercise is to focus on a single event such as the sad story of Little-faith or the life story of Hopeful or the behavior of Ignorance and analyze in detail what we learn about the Christian life in it. Then we can do the same for another segment of the chapter.

PART 1, CHAPTER 10
Entering the Celestial City

Plot Summary

In the final chapter of part 1 of *Pilgrim's Progress* the protagonist finally attains the goal of his quest. The chapter unfolds in three phases: passage through Beulah land, crossing the river of death, and being welcomed into the Celestial City. Beulah is another archetypal good place—a place where the "air was very sweet and pleasant" and "where were orchards, vineyards, and gardens." Furthermore, the view of Heaven is so resplendent that the pilgrims find their senses overwhelmed by the sight.

Between the pilgrims and the Celestial City runs a very deep river without a bridge over it. The pilgrims "addressed themselves to the water," and Christian struggles to maintain his footing and his courage. He is even fearful that he will die in the river. But Hopeful keeps encouraging him, and after his shaky start Christian finds that "the rest of the river was but shallow."

Then we come to the grand finale—the entrance in Heaven. Two Shining Ones are imme-

> The river of death (which incidentally is not so named in the text) is one of Bunyan's most evocative inventions. From time immemorial, the passage from this life to the life beyond has been pictured as a river that must be crossed. The physical difficulties that Christian experiences as he wades through the water are symbolic of the doubts and fears that accompany human death. The effect is moving and numinous.

49

> It is a time-honored strategy for storytellers who write about a journey to a perfect place (whether Paradise or Heaven) to lavish attention on creating a sense of anticipation for the place that lies ahead. Bunyan exploits the technique of the gradual approach to the full in a long paragraph that begins, "The talk they had with the Shining Ones was about the glory of the place." C. S. Lewis's commentary on the gradual approach to Paradise in Milton's *Paradise Lost* applies to this passage in *Pilgrim's Progress* as well: "In this kind of poetry the poet's battles are mainly won in advance. If he can give us the idea of increasing expectancy, . . . then, when at last he has to make a show of describing the garden itself, we shall be already conquered. He is doing his work *now* so that when the climax comes we shall actually do the work for ourselves" (*A Preface to Paradise Lost* [New York: Oxford University Press, 1942], 49).

diately present after the pilgrims cross the river. Christian and Hopeful find themselves speeding toward the Celestial City. Bunyan is in the tradition of great fiction writers like Dante and Milton who create a sense of anticipation about Heaven as travelers journey toward it but have not yet arrived. When the pilgrims approach the gate, they are surrounded by a throng of heavenly residents who function as a grand welcoming committee. Upon passing through the gate, Christian and Hopeful are "transfigured, and . . . had raiment put on that shone like gold." After a very brief description of Heaven, Bunyan concludes his story of Christian's pilgrimage with the expulsion of Ignorance when he attempts to enter the Celestial City.

Commentary

The goal of Christian's quest has permeated the story so completely that we enter the final chapter thinking that we know exactly how the story will end. Perhaps for that very reason, Bunyan springs so many surprises on us in the last chapter that at some level the story can be said to have a surprise ending.

Of course some of our expectations are fulfilled. The goal toward which the plot has been oriented from the beginning is climactically achieved as Christian enters the Celestial City. Furthermore, we expect to find the approach to Heaven to be a foretaste of final bliss, and the place called Beulah meets that expectation. Nor are we surprised by an angelic escort that accompanies the two pilgrims on the final leg of their journey. We know that Heaven has a gate, and we are hardly surprised by the throng of saints that is waiting for the arrival of the pilgrims. Bunyan's Heaven is filled with musical sound, as we fully expected. And of course Heaven shines like the sun and has streets of gold, and the book of Revelation has long since conditioned us to expect saints "with crowns on their heads, palms in their hands, and golden harps to sing praises withal."

But counteracting the effect of the familiar is a host of surprises. The first is the threatening river of death. Once the pilgrims enter Beulah land, we expect an easy transition to Heaven, but the river is instead the last (and very great) obstacle on Christian's pilgrimage. Christian is overwhelmed with fear as he stands in the river. He "was much in the troublesome thoughts of the sins that he had committed." He begins to sink, and the crossing of the river becomes yet another of the narrow escapes in this adventure story.

Secondly, in a story where the Celestial City has been constantly kept before us, it is truly surprising that the description of it is so brief at the story's conclusion. We get just a few familiar details, and then the description unexpectedly ends after just half a page. Bunyan may be drawing upon a very old convention known as an inexpressibility motif, based on the premise that something is so beautiful or wonderful, or belongs so thoroughly to a transcendent "other" world, that the reality of it cannot be expressed in human language. But the storyteller almost always makes it explicit that this is what is governing the account, and Bunyan offers no explanation along those lines.

A third surprise is that the story ends not with the entry of Christian into Heaven but with the expulsion of Ignorance from Heaven. The final scene is not one of acceptance but of rejection. The penultimate sentence in the book (followed by the

> The welcome of the believer into Heaven is one of the great subjects of Christian writers through the centuries, starting with the Bible. If you know of parallel passages in other works of literature, using them as collaborative reading will enrich your experience of Bunyan's picture. Three good examples are these: John Milton, "Lycidas" (lines 172–85) and Sonnet 14; George Herbert, "Love. III." Of course the Bible is the definitive text; relevant texts are these: Matthew 25:14–21; 31–40; Revelation 21 and 22:1–5.

formula, "So I awoke, and behold it was a dream") is the stern warning, "Then I saw that there was a way to hell, even from the gates of Heaven, as well as from the City of Destruction." The explanation is doubtless that throughout his writings Bunyan is very concerned to warn his readers about false consolations and to steer them away from religious attitudes and practices that deceive people into thinking that they are bound for glory when they are not.

> Storytellers often close their stories by echoing the beginning. The effect is that of completing a circle. The opening sentence of part 1 of *Pilgrim's Progress* informs us that the narrator lay down to sleep and "dreamed a dream." The last sentence reads, "So I awoke, and behold it was a dream." The first main event is Christian's escape from the City of Destruction. The next-to-last sentence of the book is, "Then I saw that there was a way to hell, even from the gates of Heaven, as well as from the City of Destruction."

For Reflection or Discussion

As we read a long story such as *Pilgrim's Progress*, it is natural to formulate expectations in our minds as to how the story will end. When we reach the end, therefore, we can reflect on how the conclusion of the story matches the expectations that we have formulated and how it fails to meet those expectations. This principle can be applied with good effect as we ponder the conclusion of part 1 of *Pilgrim's Progress*. A second good exercise is to compare Bunyan's vision of entering Heaven with the Bible's pictures of Heaven. What did Bunyan choose to omit? What did he include? Additionally, the success of Bunyan's story about Christian's journey to Heaven depends on the storyteller's ability to make the goal of his pilgrim's quest fully satisfactory; how do you rate Bunyan's success at making good on the task that the story by its very nature imposed on him? Is the goal Christian reaches worthy of the arduous journey that precedes it?

PART 2, CHAPTER 1
Christiana Resolves to Flee the City of Destruction

Plot Summary

To introduce the story of Christian's family (companion story to that of Christian in part 1), Bunyan hit upon something ingenious: he imagines the first-person narrator as traveling to the City of Destruction to learn what became of Christian's family after his escape from his hometown. The narrator claims to have taken up lodging a mile from the town where the first half of *Pilgrim's Progress* began. Of course the narrator falls asleep and dreams (just as he did at the beginning of part 1), and by means of this transition we are propelled into part 2 of *Pilgrim's Progress*.

Then Bunyan springs another surprise on us. Instead of picturing the narrator as dreaming the action and remaining outside of it as an observer, Bunyan now places the narrator inside the dream, conversing directly with a character in the story. The first thing that happens to the narrator as participant in his dream is an encounter with Mr. Sagacity, of whom he asks a series of questions. He asks first whether Mr. Sagacity has heard of a former member of the town named Christian. Mr. Sagacity answers affirmatively. Then the narrator asks what Christian's wife, Christiana, and her sons plan to do. Mr. Sagacity replies that Christiana has resolved to follow in the steps of her husband.

Mr. Sagacity offers to tell the narrator the story of Christiana and her four sons, and after that the narrative flows as part 1 had done—as a story told within the framework of a dream. The action be-

Parts 1 and 2 of *Pilgrim's Progress* fall into a very old artistic tradition known as "companion pieces." A famous example is the two portrait paintings of a boy and girl known as *Blue Boy* and *Pinkie*, which in reproductions often hang side by side on the wall in homes (the originals, painted by different painters, are at the Huntington Art Gallery in California). John Milton wrote companion poems entitled *L'Allegro* ["Mirth"] and *Il Penseroso* ["Pensiveness"]. Part 2 of *Pilgrim's Progress* will yield its literary pleasures if we keep our antennae up for "echoes with a difference" in relation to part 1.

gins with Christiana becoming convicted by the thought that her husband had been right about the need to escape from the City of Destruction. After a tormented night in which she sees her husband "in a place of bliss," she wakes the next morning and hears a knock at her door. The name of the visitor is Secret, sent from "the Merciful One" to assure Christiana that God "is a God ready to forgive." In fact, Secret hands over a letter from her husband's King, who "would have her do as did Christian her husband." Christiana gathers her sons around her and tells them to "pack up and begone to the gate that leads to the Celestial Country."

Commentary

The first thing to get into our heads if we wish to relish part 2 of *Pilgrim's Progress* is that this story will not be a rerun of part 1. The second important thing is to realize that the mere fact that part 2 is less well known than part 1 does not make it an inferior work of literature. The antidote to these two misconceptions is to read part 2 with the same care that part 1 has always elicited from readers. The story of Christiana is a companion story to part 1. Although part 2 tells us about visits to many of the same places visited by Christian on his pilgrimage, in all of the parallel episodes in part 2 Bunyan invents something entirely different. The most noteworthy thing about the two parts of *Pilgrim's Progress* is not their similarities but their differences. The two parts are complementary to each other; without the other, both stories would be incomplete. Additionally, Bunyan's storytelling genius and skill with spiritual allegory did not desert him when he composed part 2 six years after the publication of part 1.

The genre of companion pieces is a specific manifestation of an even broader artistic principle. In the introduction to his book *Reflections on the Psalms*, C. S. Lewis comments on this principle in a discussion of the verse form of Hebrew parallelism: "The principle of art has been defined by someone as 'the same in the other.' Thus in a country dance you take three steps and then three steps again. That is the same. But the first three are to the right and the second three to the left. That is the other."

C. S. Lewis's story *The Great Divorce* makes excellent collaborative reading for the opening chapter of part 2 (and indeed for all of *Pilgrim's Progress*). In *Pilgrim's Progress*, Christiana has a vision of her glorified husband in Heaven; in Lewis's story, various shining figures from Heaven make a final appeal to a busload of family members and acquaintances from Hell to choose Heaven (only one does). The motif is the same in both stories: the bliss enjoyed by citizens of Heaven beckons people in their lost state to repent.

Bunyan serves notice on us immediately that he plans to be as original and inventive in part 2 as he was in part 1. The opening ploy of imagining that the narrator of part 1 makes a trip to the City of Destruction to see what has transpired in the intervening years is clever. So is the daring move of making the narrator a participant in the dream that Bunyan uses as the framework for narrating his story.

Chapter 1 of part 2 belongs to a literary genre known as the "story of resolve," in which a character ponders his or her situation and comes to a courageous decision to make a radical change. In keeping with the principle of "the same in the other" (see marginal note on page 54 for more), the thing that initially seizes our notice is what is identical in the opening scenes of both parts of *Pilgrim's Progress*. Both husband and wife come to a resolution to flee the City of Destruction, representative of the lost state. That part is "the same." But the differences keep multiplying. Christiana carries no burden on her back. Furthermore, she is spiritually responsible for her children and does not make a solitary decision to leave. Christiana has a guide to follow in the example of her husband, who made the perilous journey and is now in Heaven. And so forth.

> In keeping with the genre of the companion story, we can note the way in which the largely masculine world of part 1 is now balanced by a feminine focus in part 2. Part 2 is a woman's story. Additionally, whereas Christian left his children behind (in token of the way in which every individual needs to be converted personally), the presence of the four sons in part 2 brings a family or domestic dimension to Bunyan's story of salvation, prompting us to think about how the life of faith works along family lines as well as individually.

For Reflection or Discussion

The key to enjoying part 2 of *Pilgrim's Progress* is to realize that it is not a rerun of previous action. Instead it is a companion story to part 1. Two questions continuously lead to good analysis of part 2: (1) What is echoed from the parallel episode in part 1? (2) What innovations make the episode strikingly different from its parallel in part 1?

Additionally, the spiritual struggles of Christiana in the opening chapter fall into the theological category of conviction of sin; what familiar features of that theological reality does Bunyan put before us in this episode?

PART 2, CHAPTER 2

The Journey from the City of Destruction to the Interpreter's House

Plot Summary

Christiana and her sons have no more than made their decision to escape from the City of Destruction than they hear a knock on their door. The visitors on the doorstep are two neighbor women. One of them, Mrs. Timorous, reviles Christiana for supposed madness in undertaking a journey well known in the town for its dangers. The other person at the door, Mercy, decides to walk a short distance with Christiana. Mrs. Timorous returns to her home, where she is visited by a very bad lot of neighbors who have such evocative names as Mrs. Lightmind, Mrs. Know-nothing, and Madam Wanton.

Meanwhile, Christiana and Mercy proceed on the King's High-way, with Christiana (who has a letter of invitation from the King of the Celestial Country) promising to intercede on Mercy's behalf at the wicket-gate. The travelers are at first stymied by the Slough of Despond, but they manage rather easily by stepping on the stones that had been ordered by "command of the King to make this place for pilgrims good." At this point we read

---

When the neighbor women call on Christiana, we are strongly aware that part 2 shows a feminine concern in Bunyan's choice of story material. This extends to Christiana's traveling companion, a young woman named Mercy. On the other hand, the fact that Christiana travels through the same terrain that her husband did (starting with the Slough of Despond) alerts us that the Christian life in its essence transcends gender.

that "now Mr. Sagacity left me to dream out my dream by myself," and thereafter we return to the narrative mode that prevailed in part 1.

The next milestone on the journey is arrival at the wicket-gate. Christiana knocks and hears a barking dog that terrifies her and her children. But the Keeper of the gate silences the dog and opens the gate. Mercy trembles outside the gate, fearing God's rejection because she does not possess a letter of invitation from the King. But she eventually knocks at the gate and is also admitted. The Keeper of the gate speaks encouraging words to the pilgrims.

When the pilgrims request the Keeper of the gate to do something about the terrible dog, they are told that the dog belongs to the owner of a nearby castle. They further learn that the barking serves the useful purpose of frightening true pilgrims into a courageous resolve to press forward to Heaven. Then another terror is thrust before us: Christiana's children innocently gather fruit from the branches of the enemy's trees that lean over the wall. Two "very ill-favoured" men appear and threaten the women and children. The women shriek in terror and are rescued by the Reliever. Christiana recounts a dream that she had back in the City of Destruction of these very men, "plotting how they might prevent my salvation." With a little more journeying the group arrives at the House Beautiful.

> The Slough of Despond symbolizes the despair that easily overwhelms the person who is conscious of sin but not yet fully established in the life of faith in Christ. This group of six travelers manages to get through the slough with relative ease because they followed Mercy's advice and "looked well to the steps." In a marginal note in the section of part 1 where Christian flounders in the Slough of Despond, the steps were identified as God's promises.

Commentary

The opening scene of resolve is now followed by a scene of leave taking or departure. The conventions have existed from time immemorial. Neighbors hear about the decision to leave, and they pay a visit either to help or to hinder the departure.

Mrs. Timorous and Mercy function as foils to each other, with one being impervious to the danger represented by the sinful and lost state and the other feeling the beginning stirrings of the spiritual quest for salvation.

The first leg of the journey provides a good test of generalizations made above about the principle of companion stories. The pilgrims reach the same Slough of Despond that Christian encountered in part 1, but they are not overwhelmed by the bog as Christian was. The pilgrims arrive at the wicket-gate, as Christian had done, but there the likeness ends. Instead of flying arrows that deter pilgrims from proceeding, we have a barking dog. The entrance of a solitary pilgrim through the gate is here rendered complex by multiple entrances, including the delayed entrance by the fearful Mercy. In traversing the same space, Christian had been tempted by such alluring figures as Mr. Legality and Mr. Worldly-wise, whereas Christiana and her fellow travelers need to be rescued from a physical scuffle with two bullying ruffians.

> The detail of the barking dog that terrifies the travelers serves notice on us that Bunyan's commitment to the genre of the adventure story (and its subcategory the horror story) remains alive and well in part 2. It is also a reminder that despite the fantasy [unlifelike] elements that make up the bulk of *Pilgrim's Progress*, there is also a strain of everyday realism in the story. Everyone knows about a neighbor's terrifying dog.

For Reflection or Discussion

At the level of the "story as story," we can profitably ponder the means by which Bunyan makes the action come alive in our imagination. What makes this chapter good story material? At the level of spiritual allegory, we need to explore what the various experiences of the pilgrims embody about the first stirrings of faith in a soul headed for conversion. Another way to approach this is to begin with the premise that in part 2 (as in part 1) Bunyan aims to recount what in theology is called the "order of salvation." What are the first steps in that sequence?

PART 2, CHAPTER 3
Interpreter's House

Plot Summary

Arriving at the door of the house of Interpreter, Christiana knocks and finds the door opened by a damsel named Innocent. When the residents of the house learn that the very person who earlier had refused to leave the City of Destruction is now a pilgrim, "they leaped for joy." A joyous scene of welcome ensues. When Christian had visited the house of Interpreter, he had been shown various paintings, objects, and persons for his instruction, and the same motif is followed with Christiana, but the details are different.

The first example is a room where a man with a "muck-rake" [rake] keeps looking downward while someone [Christ] stands over him offering him a crown. Neglecting even to look up, the man keeps raking "the straws, the small sticks, and dust of the floor." Next, a spacious room with only an ugly spider in it symbolizes the venom of sin that can take hold in the most promising of places (even a king's palace). Elsewhere a chicken symbolizes a virtuous king, a sheep that accepts his death calmly signals the need to endure difficulty without complaint, a garden with flowers illustrates the need to bear fruit, and a robin serves as an emblem for nominal rather than genuine Christians. Thereafter the Interpreter recites a catalog of proverbs.

After an afternoon of instruction, the pilgrims sit down to a meal and recount what has happened thus far on their journey. After a night of sleep, the usual rituals of hospitality unfold—a bath, the

---

Virtually the first event to occur after the pilgrims enter the house is a visit to the "significant rooms" of Interpreter that were given detailed attention when Christian visited the house: "the man in the cage, the man and his dream, . . . together with the rest of those things that were then so profitable to Christian." Obviously Bunyan wants us to recall the first visit to Interpreter's House, but just as obviously he intends to avoid boring us with repetition.

Like John Milton, Bunyan was a master at taking a single verse from the Bible (such as Proverbs 30:28, that "the spider taketh hold with her hands, and is in kings' palaces" [KJV]) and inventing a whole event based on it. Analyzing this strategy shows two things: (1) the resourcefulness of Bunyan's creative imagination, and (2) glimpses into Bunyan as a biblical exegete (interpreter of the biblical text).

donning of fresh garments, and the setting forth with an armed protector named Great-heart.

Commentary

Any fear that a second visit to Interpreter's house might be a mere rerun of Christian's visit is quickly dispelled. The only repeated elements are the rituals of hospitality that unfold and the instructive purpose that governs the visit. Beyond that, the invented details and the lessons taught and learned are complementary to what Christian experienced in the same house.

A good working premise for this episode is that Bunyan wished to show the range of categories about which a Christian needs to know in order to live a godly life. For example, some of the details are warnings about what to avoid (worldly mindedness in the muck-raker, sin as symbolized by the spider). The political life is included as well (the Heaven-looking chicken as symbol of a godly king). Elsewhere we catch glimpses of the moral life (the varied flowers that stand in peace among themselves).

For Reflection or Discussion

There are so many individual details in Interpreter's house that we can lose our way in it. We need to progress slowly through the chapter, allowing the individual lessons to sink in. If the varied details can be assumed to be a composite portrait of essential information about living the Christian life, what generalizations can we make about that subject? For you personally, what new insights about the Christian life are embedded in the episode of Interpreter's house? Are there surprises?

Another inventive thing that Bunyan does in *Pilgrim's Progress* is to recount an event as he saw it in his "dream," and then have a character in the story give his or her account of that event to a listener later in the story. For example, we view the story of Mercy from the outside when the narrator tells about her decision to continue on the journey with Christiana, but seated at the supper table in Interpreter's House we listen to Mercy give her own explanation of how she happens to be on the pilgrimage.

PART 2, CHAPTER 4
Journey to the House Beautiful

Plot Summary

The six pilgrims set out from the house of Interpreter under the protection of the soldier-in-armor Great-heart. When Christiania asks for an explanation of what it means that she will "have pardon by word and deed," Great-heart responds with a long theological explanation of the righteousness of Christ and its imparting to believers. With this long instructive passage behind us, the perilous journey continues.

The first terrifying detail is the sight of the corpses of Simple, Sloth, and Presumption hanging up in irons beside the road. By the time Great-heart explains how bad the three had been, we are resigned to their deaths. After drinking some restorative water from a spring, the pilgrims proceed up the Hill Difficulty. During the climb, the group rests in "the Prince's arbour."

Repeating Christian's mistake of losing his roll, Christiana leaves her bottle of refreshing spirits in the same place.

Passing the place where Mistrust and Timorous had attempted to dissuade Christian from going forward, the pilgrims come within sight of the lions that had terrified Christian. Great-heart is courageous, but a giant named Grim threatens the travelers. Great-heart hacks the Giant Grim to pieces in single combat, and the group proceeds to the Porter's Lodge of the House Beautiful. To the dismay of the pilgrims, Great-heart announces that he must return to his lord that night. (Great-heart later returns to guide the pilgrims when they leave the House Beautiful.)

Reading about the atoning work of Christ in the relevant section of a systematic theology can serve as a guide to the discourse of Great-heart early in this chapter. If you do not have access to a book of systematic theology, reading Romans 5:18–21 is a good idea; it talks about the real righteousness of Christ and the application of that righteousness to believers who claim it by faith in Christ's substitutionary atonement. Some editions of *Pilgrim's Progress* list additional verses from the New Testament epistles.

Bunyan's allegorical names continue to be a leading feature and attraction of his story, and there is often a latent humor about them. The list of people who were derailed from the pilgrims' path by Simple, Sloth, and Presumption illustrates the technique: Slow-pace, Short-wind, No-heart, Sleepy-head, and Dull.

Commentary

The episode is divided between didactic discourse and heroic adventure. Great-heart's discourse about the real and imputed righteousness of Christ is the most explicitly theological passage in the entire book. Reading about the same subject in a book of systematic theology makes good collateral reading. The second half of the chapter is in the best tradition of romance or fantasy stories. We have such conventional features of heroic narrative as the corpses of executed criminals on public display, a spring in which the waters have supernatural powers of refreshment, a hill climbed with difficulty, a paradisal arbor, threatening lions, and a giant defeated in open combat by a heroic warrior representing the good.

For Reflection or Discussion

Great-heart's discourse on the righteousness of Christ requires careful reading and theological analysis; what specific doctrines relating to salvation does Bunyan put into the passage? When we move beyond the scene of instruction to the adventure of the journey, what narrative and fantasy details most attract your interest? What parallels from similar stories (such as the adventure stories of C. S. Lewis and J. R. R. Tolkien) provide depth of field as you bring them to bear on this part of *Pilgrim's Progress*?

The threats encountered on the trek up the Hill Difficulty are governed by Bunyan's sure instinct for variety of adventure. The rigors of the climb are offset by the refreshing arbor. The realism of the physical journey is set against the fantasy of lions and a giant who is subdued in single combat. That nightmare experience, in turn, is balanced by the travelers' arrival at a safe house whose porter bears the reassuring name Mr. Watchful.

The giant-killing motif is a favorite with storytellers. The historical prototype is David's killing of Goliath; reading that story in 1 Samuel 17 makes good parallel reading to Great-heart's conquest of the Giant Grim. Then we can add fictional accounts of the same motif. Smiting off an arm or head is a virtual necessity for a respectable battle in the heroic tradition.

PART 2, CHAPTER 5
Visit to the House Beautiful

Plot Summary
The porter Mr. Watchful asks Christiana the usual questions about who the travelers are, after which he invites the group into the house. A meal ensues, and then heavenly music fills the house. In the morning, Mercy tells about having dreamt that an angel led her to Heaven. Prudence, Piety, and Charity invite the group to stay longer, and the travelers accept the invitation. Prudence then asks catechism questions of the children, who acquit themselves well.

A visitor named Mr. Brisk, who "pretended to religion," arrives and attempts to court the young woman Mercy. When Mercy shows herself exemplary in Christian behavior, Mr. Brisk loses interest in her. The next crisis occurs when Matthew falls ill, requiring a visit from the physician, named Dr. Skill. When questioned, Matthew admits to having eaten the fruit that hung from a branch that leaned over the wall as the group passed. Dr. Skill prescribes a pill that heals Matthew. He also supplies Christiana with boxes of pills for the rest of the trip.

The recovered Matthew asks Prudence a series of questions about the spiritual life and is duly instructed. After a month at the House Beautiful, the travelers make motions of wishing to resume their journey, so the residents of House Beautiful follow a custom of giving a departing group something on which to meditate on the way. The group is led to a place where they see Jacob's ladder, with angels ascending and descending, and then to a place

C. S. Lewis once described the medieval imagination as so didactic ("having the intention to teach") that readers back then were always up for a passage of straight instruction dropped into a story; in Lewis's words, if a writer were so generous "as to give you an extra bit of doctrine . . . , who would be so churlish as to refuse it on the pedantic ground of irrelevance?" Bunyan's Puritan imagination is of exactly that didactic nature. There is no other way to account for the heavy dose of doctrinal material in this chapter.

with a golden anchor hanging. Next the group goes up the mountain on which Abraham offered Isaac. After a return to the house, Mr. Great-heart arrives with symbolic wine and food for the trip. The group leaves under the protection of Great-heart. A final event is Piety's giving Christiana "a scheme" of all things seen at House Beautiful so she can bring the visit to remembrance.

Commentary

The narrative principle governing the episode is "the same in the other." The house and its residents are exactly the same as when Christian had visited the house in part 1. In fact, a useful exercise is to take a quick look at the earlier visit to refresh the memory about what happened to Christian on his visit. When we do that, it is obvious that Bunyan did everything necessary to avoid duplication. The visitors are different. The attempted courtship of Mercy and illness of Matthew are domestic touches totally unlike Christian's experiences at the house. So are the interludes of Mercy's dream of Heaven and the children's catechism lesson. Bunyan's instinct for variety of adventure is alive and well in this chapter.

On the other hand, certain other things remain constant across the two visits. One is that the purpose of visiting the house is to experience refreshment to offset the rigors of the journey. A second purpose of a visit to a house in a travel story such as this is instructive, as the travelers receive the information they need to complete their mission. Since Bunyan is telling a story about the need to persist in the Christian life and thereby attain Heaven, we need to ponder what the instructive details tell us about those topics.

Mr. Brisk, for all his unworthiness as a suitor to Mercy, introduces a surprising romantic love motif into the story. The archetype that unfolds is well known in literature—the virtuous young woman who attracts the attention of a worldly and unworthy man. The placing of this event here makes the eventual love relationship between Mercy and Christiana's son Matthew seem a little less implausible than it would otherwise be. As a person who "pretended to religion" but "stuck very close to the world," Mr. Brisk represents a type that the Puritans particularly disliked.

For Reflection or Discussion

A good avenue toward relishing Bunyan's story is to pay attention to his inventiveness in thinking up interesting narrative events. An adventure story needs to win us with the cleverness of story material; how does Bunyan satisfy that expectation in this episode? Second, a main purpose of *Pilgrim's Progress* is to lead us to contemplate the nature of the Christian life and the doctrinal content of the Christian faith. Why does Bunyan give us such details as Mercy's vision of Heaven, the place of Jacob's ladder, the golden anchor, and the mountain where Abraham offered his son Isaac? Why these particular details?

PART 2, CHAPTER 6
Journey through the Valley of Humiliation

Plot Summary

As the journey resumes, the pilgrims enter the same Valley of Humiliation where Christian had engaged in a life-or-death battle with the monster Apollyon. But Bunyan springs a surprise on us: this valley is actually a good place for "those that love a pilgrim's life." Accordingly, the valley is described as a paradisal place of meadows and lilies. But in keeping with the rhythm of a travel story, this pastoral oasis is only a prelude to another round of terrifying ordeals on the way.

As the group comes to "the snares," they see a man named Heedless "cast into the ditch on the left hand, with his flesh all rent and torn." But this

---

The Valley of Humiliation had been such a threatening ordeal for Christian in part 1 that we can scarcely avoid being shocked by the reversal that occurs here. A pillar commemorating Christian's experience gives us the explanation that we need: "Let Christian's slips, before he came hither, and the battles that he met with in this place, be a warning to those that come after." In other words, the nature of one's experience in the Valley of Humiliation depends on the spiritual state of the person. We can infer that Christian had been beset with sins in a way that Christiana is not. We might note in this regard that Christiana

Bunyan's "The Pilgrim's Progress"

finds her pilgrimage to the Celestial City a great deal easier than it was for Christian.

When James suddenly becomes sick and revives when he takes a pill given by Dr. Skill at the House Beautiful, we find ourselves in the familiar fantasy-story world of magical potions—like Lucy's cordial in the Narnia stories. Depending on how many fantasy stories you have read, other examples might be plentiful.

Bunyan's story is notable for the range of story materials and motifs that he incorporates. Immediately following the paragraph of the fairy-tale motif of miraculous cures, we find a paragraph rooted in the Bible. When a menacing fiend suddenly vanishes before the pilgrims, we have seen an instance of the promise of James 4:7: "Resist the devil, and he will flee from you." As Charles Spurgeon once noted, Bunyan's remarkable acquaintance with every part of the Bible is always coming to the surface as he composes his story; Spurgeon's oft-quoted statement was, "Prick him anywhere; and ... the very essence of the Bible flows from him. He cannot speak

initial terror is minor compared to the giant Maul who suddenly emerges from a cave. Maul's specialty is kidnapping women and children and carrying them away from God's kingdom. Another single combat ensues, with Great-heart eventually smiting "the head of the giant from his shoulders." The travelers sit down to eat and drink. Shortly thereafter they meet one of Bunyan's most attractive characters, Mr. Honest.

After an exchange of pleasantries between Great-heart and Honest, the group continues forward. Great-heart asks if Honest knows about Mr. Fearing, who came from Honest's hometown of Stupidity. This leads to an extended account from Great-heart (guide to the Celestial City) of the difficulties of leading Mr. Fearing on the pilgrimage to Heaven. This narrative of Mr. Fearing leads logically to a discussion among the travelers about the reasons for spiritual fear and the bad effects of it. That, in turn, telescopes into an analysis of spiritual detriment of being self-indulgent, as embodied in the life and attitudes of Mr. Self-will. This segment of the journey reaches an expected conclusion when the pilgrims arrive at an inn.

Commentary

This episode is one of the longer ones in *Pilgrim's Progress*, and we can say of it that it has "something for everyone." The first thing to grasp is that in effect we get two stories—one of the pilgrims as they move through the Valley of Humiliation and beyond, and the second is a mini-narrative of Mr. Fearing's pilgrimage from his hometown of Stupidity (which is even "worse than is the City of Destruction") to the Celestial City. A second helpful tip is to be aware that as we hear the stories of various pilgrims, the same place names keep coming up (e.g., the Slough of Despond, the Hill Difficulty, the Valley of Humiliation), so that a kind of cumulative picture of the universal pilgrimage of life takes shape in our imaginations.

Another narrative principle to keep in mind is that storytellers organize their stories as a back-and-forth rhythm—between tension and release, for example, or between the familiar and the unfamiliar, or the expected and the unexpected or surprising. This principle is fully evident in chapter 6. We enter the Valley of Humiliation with dread, but that expectation is completely overturned when the valley is a paradise and the humiliation is given the positive twist of virtuous humility (not, as in the earlier experience of Christian, a defeat). The lush valley with a shepherd boy singing gives way to an epic-scale fight between a heroic warrior (Great-heart) and a villainous giant. The now-familiar cast of characters (Christiana's family, Mercy, and the guide Great-heart) is suddenly enlarged by the emergence of Old Honest.

The large amount of space given to the "story within a story" of Mr. Fearing's pilgrimage signals that it was important to Bunyan's design. The most important function of Mr. Fearing's pilgrimage is that it adds a further story of pilgrimage. As we progress through Bunyan's story, we keep getting glimpses of various people's spiritual journeys, and the message that is sent by this cumulative metanarrative ("big overarching story") is that the journey from destruction to salvation is common to all who achieve Heaven. There is one way to Heaven, but each believer must experience that way personally. Additionally, the name Mr. Fearing makes the account of his difficult journey

without quoting a text, for his soul is full of the Word of God."

Bunyan's *Pilgrim's Progress* is often contrasted to another spiritual narrative that he wrote, namely, *The Holy War*. It is common to drive a wedge between the two on the ground that one deals with pilgrimage and the other with war. The situation is not quite that simple, however, as the full-scale single combat between Great-heart and the giant Maul shows. Anyone who reads *Pilgrim's Progress* in an illustrated edition can scarcely avoid being surprised by how many of the illustrations portray a warrior in armor.

The story of Mr. Fearing (narrated by Great-heart, who guided him on his pilgrimage) is a suspense story with a surprise ending. The suspense lies in our expectation that such a timid and nonassertive person as Mr. Fearing could not possibly persist on the pilgrimage. We keep expecting him to fall out of the journey, and suspense begins to build regarding when and how he will meet his end. But for all his ineptitude as a traveler and spiritual pilgrim Mr. Fearing never quits the journey. We are

Bunyan's "The Pilgrim's Progress"

surprised to learn that he does actually make it into the Celestial City, and even more surprised when Great-heart confides that he "never had doubt about him," despite the burden he was to himself and others.

The primary reason Christiana has an easier time on her pilgrimage than Christian had on his is the fact that Great-heart serves as her guide and protector. Great-heart belongs to a timeless type known as the traveler's guide and companion. The function of that guide is always the same: to inform the traveler, to offer advice, to lead the way, and when necessary to protect the traveler against foes.

through life a case study in the bad effects of being fearful and anxious instead of confident in the strength of God.

In keeping with the narrative premise of the whole book—to give a comprehensive picture of the Christian life—the added story of Mr. Self-will takes the analysis of the spiritual life in a different direction. As we listen to the pilgrims analyze the bad effects of Mr. Self-will's philosophy of life, we are led to ponder the ways in which sensual indulgence can keep a person from attaining Heaven.

For Reflection or Discussion

Again in this episode we are reminded of events and places that we encountered in part 1. Places visited by Christian are also visited by Christiana and her family, and then Mr. Fearing's story of his pilgrimage provides yet another version of the general paradigm. To fully master *Pilgrim's Progress*, we need to draw a map (however rudimentary) of the places on the journey, along with the nature of the places and the events that happen in them. To complete such a map requires piecing together details from various parts of the story, and this is an excellent impetus to close reading of the text.

Of course in Bunyan's story the physical level symbolizes spiritual realities. So once we have the master plan of the journey before us, we can analyze what the story embodies and teaches about the Christian's life in this world. What are the pitfalls that keep one from the kingdom, and what are the virtues that Christians can exercise to overcome the obstacles to godliness?

Bunyan's "The Pilgrim's Progress"

PART 2, CHAPTER 7

At the Inn of Gaius

Plot Summary

The pilgrims arrive at the house of an innkeeper named Gaius. As the rituals of hospitality unfold, Gaius shares the information that Christian (Christiana's husband) belongs to a distinguished ancestry that originally came from Antioch and that includes such martyrs as Stephen and the apostles. When the conversation turns to the need to perpetuate the faith from one generation to the next, Gaius encourages Christiana to "look out some damsels for her sons." This is put into immediate effect when Mercy and Matthew (oldest son of Christiana) become a couple, with the added information that "in process of time they were married." Gaius climaxes the event by delivering a speech in praise of women.

When evening arrives, a sumptuous feast is provided for the pilgrims. A request to stay a month so that Matthew and Mercy might be married is granted. After supper, the children sleep while the adults spend the night in spiritual conversation. After breakfast the next morning, Great-heart seeks an adventure in keeping with his martial nature. He walks out to the cave of a villainous giant named Slay-good and cuts off his head. Great-heart's entourage also rescues a pilgrim named Mr. Feeble-mind, who narrates how he came to be under the control of Slay-good.

Before the pilgrims leave the inn of Gaius, Matthew and Mercy are married, and so are Phoebe (daughter of Gaius) and James (another of the sons of Christiana). These momentous events

Bunyan's account of Christian's ancestry is a truly inventive touch. The foundation is that when Bunyan decided to call his protagonist Christian, the name itself made Bunyan's pilgrim the prototypical or universal Christian. We read in Acts 11:26 that disciples of Jesus were first called Christians in Antioch, so Bunyan makes that the place from which Christian's lineage sprang. By then placing martyrs in Christian's lineage, we are to understand the strength of commitment that has characterized the list of descendants.

The impromptu praise of women (technically belonging to the genre of the encomium) has all the earmarks of Puritan praises of virtuous women. The real-life model on which Bunyan draws is almost certainly Puritan funeral sermons for women. These sermons always moved from an exposition of an appropriate biblical text to an elaborate praise of godly women in general and the deceased woman in particular. The praise of godly women, in turn, took exactly the same form as Gaius's discourse—a survey of biblical examples.

are narrated in a single sentence, and space is lavished instead on other happenings that occur at the leave taking. When Mr. Feeble-mind makes motions to stay at the inn, Great-heart convinces him to proceed on the pilgrimage. Then a surprise is visited on us by the arrival of Mr. Ready-to-halt on crutches. The names of these two characters make them unlikely candidates for the rigors of the pilgrimage, but they are incorporated into the group, trudging behind the strong ones.

Commentary

If we take stock of Bunyan's story up to this point, it is obvious that most of the action falls into a small number of repeated "type scenes." We owe this formula to literary scholar Robert Alter. A type scene is a set of common ingredients that keeps coming up in a given situation, whether in literature or real life. The type scene reenacted at the inn of Gaius is the scene of hospitality extended to weary travelers. The moment the pilgrims arrive at the inn of Gaius, we know what will unfold: arriving at the door, entering the house or inn, appearance of the innkeeper or master of the house, assigning of rooms to the guests, inquiry about who the travelers are, conversation between host and guests (including questions about the journey), eating a meal, sleep, entertainment (loosely defined) of the visitors, and eventual leave taking. Robert Alter refers to type scenes as "the enabling context" of a story, in this case a story of pilgrimage. In other words, we expect a certain pattern to unfold and are delighted when a storyteller meets our expectations.

But the type scene is only half of the equation. Great storytellers invent something original and

---

Pilgrim's Progress is a work of the folk imagination, and once we grant that premise, there is no reason to be surprised by the riddling session that enters the story when Gaius shows signs of drowsiness during the night of conversation. Primitive or "folk" cultures love the riddle as a literary form. Some of the parables and sayings of Jesus in the Gospels are riddles, as signaled by such formulas as "He who has ears to hear, let him hear," or, "What do you think?" The most famous riddling contest in modern literature is the one between Bilbo Baggins and Gollum in Tolkien's *The Hobbit*.

impose it on the familiar template. This is where Bunyan shows his genius. We are not surprised to learn that Christian stayed here on his pilgrimage, but the information about Christian's distinguished ancestry is as surprising to us as it is to Christiana. Even more unexpected is the engagement of Mercy and Matthew, which expands into an encomium in praise of women by Gaius.

The all-night conversation by the adults is a novel version of the conventional motif of entertainment of visitors. Equally surprising is the sudden riddling contest that is sprung on Gaius when he shows signs of drowsiness. Additionally, the whole aura of happenings at the inn has been so religiously oriented that we are caught off guard by the spectacle of Great-heart being so "good at his weapons" that after breakfast he wants to venture forth and see if he can defeat a villain or two.

A final literary feature of this chapter emerges when Mr. Feeble-mind tells the story of his wanderings and mishaps on the way. The Puritans elevated the genre of spiritual autobiography (the story of one's personal spiritual history) to a place of central importance. Feeble-mind's story of spiritual failings is a religious autobiography in a fictional mode. Furthermore, as the varied stories of pilgrims accumulate in *Pilgrim's Progress*, it is obvious that Bunyan is not telling the story of just one or two pilgrims but of many. *Pilgrim's Progress* finally takes shape as an anthology of pilgrim stories.

For Reflection or Discussion

What familiar features of the traveler's visit to a house are reenacted? How does Bunyan manage his story in such a way as to infuse a spiritual fla-

---

Even though the pilgrimages of Christian and Christiana follow the same general itinerary, the two stories have a much different flavor. In part 1, pilgrimage is depicted as something only the strong can achieve. In keeping with the feminine and domestic world in which we move in part 2, the quest for Heaven is portrayed as something that even the weak can achieve. We have already seen one example in the life story of Mr. Fearing, who entered Heaven almost in spite of himself. Here in chapter 7, we get another memorable picture of the same spiritual reality when Feeble-mind and Ready-to-halt are allowed to join the group that departs from the inn of Gaius.

vor into the conventions of a travel story? How does the autobiography of Feeble-mind teach us by negative example how to live the Christian life?

PART 2, CHAPTER 8
Conclusion of the Perilous Journey

Plot Summary

The story of the journey from the inn of Gaius to the river of death is the most packed with different adventures in the entire *Pilgrim's Progress*. When the group arrives at the town of Vanity (site of Vanity Fair), Great-heart proposes that they spend the night at the house of Mnason. The neighbors are summoned (people with names such as Contrite, Holy-man, Love-saint), and conversation on religious matters ensues. The travelers stay "a great while," as attested by the fact that another of Christiana's sons, Samuel, marries Grace, the daughter of Mnason. Mercy spends the time laboring "much for the poor." During the stay a monster comes out of the woods and is scared off by Great-heart and others.

When the group resumes traveling, they pass the places that we read about in part 1—the Hill Lucre, the Delectable Mountains, By-path Meadow, Doubting Castle. At the Delectable Mountains, shepherds provide a feast for the pilgrims. The shepherds take the pilgrims to Mount Marvel, Mount Innocent, and Mount Charity. As the journey continues to unfold, the travelers meet Valiant-for-truth, another of Bunyan's stalwarts.

Mr. Valiant-for-truth is one of Bunyan's most famous and endearing characters. He is noteworthy for his courage in pursuing the Christian life. He is an arch-Puritan in his devotion to truth and his zest for the active life. While part 2 of *Pilgrim's Progress* is generally oriented toward the spiritual lives of the needy and weak, characters like Great-heart and Valiant-for-truth balance the picture and serve as foils to the women and children and ready-to-halts of the story.

As conversation ensues, another pilgrim story (that of Valiant-for-truth) gets added to the anthology that makes up *Pilgrim's Progress*.

A new phase is reached when the group arrives at the Enchanted Ground. Mist and darkness fall on the travelers, and "the way also was here very wearisome." In keeping with the nature of this enchanted place to induce sleep, the travelers find Heedless and Too-bold asleep. At the far end of the Enchanted Ground the group meets Stand-fast. He recounts his temptation by a woman named Madame Bubble, a voluptuous woman who represents not simply sexual temptation but worldliness more generally (including the love of riches). The journey ends in the Land of Beulah, described as a kind of outpost of Heaven itself.

Commentary

Bunyan's handling of the sojourn in the town of Vanity shows more clearly than anything else in part 2 that he was intent on preventing the second part of his story from being a rerun of part 1. The town of Vanity here contains nearly none of the terror that it held for Christian and Faithful. The neighbors of Mnason are godly people (to our surprise), and the time spent in the town is on balance a peaceful interlude.

We noted earlier in this guide that stories swing like a pendulum between contrasts. The peaceful interlude in the town of Vanity is immediately set against the battle with Giant Despair at Doubting Castle. The battle is a self-respecting heroic combat, as the giantess Diffidence is cut down by Old Honest and Great-heart "severed [Giant Despair's] head from his shoulders." As is often

Madame Bubble, dubbed a witch by Great-heart, is so palpably a repulsive temptress that it would be easy to pass her off with little consideration. Yet Bunyan lavished his descriptive technique on her, intending that we take a close look at her. She is portrayed as an energetic and forceful woman. The paragraph-long catalog of how she beguiles pilgrims shows how formidable she is as a temptress. Yet the name Bubble signals how empty and insubstantial she really is.

true in heroic narrative, the defeat of a monster or tyrant is followed by the rescue of his prisoners.

Valiant-for-truth's story of his pilgrimage functions as a recap of the main action of *Pilgrim's Progress*. In a symbolic return to the beginning of *Pilgrim's Progress*, Valiant-for-truth came under conviction of sin in the same general region as the City of Destruction. He did so, moreover, when Tell-true came to his hometown and told the story of Christian's pilgrimage. As Valiant-for-truth continues his narrative, we hear of the now-familiar places on the way—the Slough of Despond, the Hill Difficulty, the Valley of Humiliation, and many more.

Knowing that the account of the journey is about to end, Bunyan gives us one last version of the staples of his travel story. The stay at Mnason's house is the last scene of hospitality extended to pilgrims on the way. The fight with Giant Despair and demolition of Doubting Castle bring the combat motif to a grand finale in the story. Valiant-for-truth's spiritual autobiography is the last pilgrim story we hear. The temptation motif also makes is final appearances. An enchanted arbor that induces sleep has been a mainstay with storytellers through the ages, and Bunyan gives us his version of it. Madame Bubble represents temptation to the gross indulgence of flesh and riches.

But Bunyan never ends with trial and struggle. The pastoral green world, which has punctuated the action, now receives its climax in the description of the Land of Beulah. Similarly, there have been numerous visions and foreshadowings of the Celestial City, but the celebratory picture at the end of this chapter tops them all with the sounds of bells and trumpets, the appearance of Shining Ones, and the smells of spices.

> The arrival in the Land of Beulah is a climactic point in the quest story of part 2. Bunyan has excelled in portraying places of respite for weary travelers, and this pastoral green world is one of his best. But the passage is not just a pastoral retreat; Bunyan introduces a riot of sounds and movement of people into the scene. A tone of celebration hovers over the episode.

For Reflection or Discussion

As we move toward the end of a travel story, we need to operate on the premise that the storyteller is not simply giving us more of the same but is choosing narrative details that possess "summing up" qualities for the story as a whole. We can analyze this last leg of the pilgrimage in light of this, theorizing about why Bunyan invented the specific details that he did for this concluding stage of his story. Related to that, it is common for storytellers to include details in the late phase of a story that remind us of events and characters that have preceded. What echoes of earlier parts of the story appear in chapter 8?

PART 2, CHAPTER 9
Saying Good-Bye to Life on Earth

Plot Summary

The chapter begins with a messenger's arrival with a letter summoning Christiana to meet her Master [God] within ten days. This produces a round of activities appropriate to a departure from this life—preparations for the journey across the river of death, pronouncement of blessing on the children, good-byes and final exchanges between Christiana and her fellow pilgrims. All of the pilgrims accompany Christiana to the river. No account is given of her actually crossing the river; instead the focus shifts to the responses of those who remain.

The concluding phase of the story is a mini-anthology of leave takings, as the remaining pilgrims

---

The summons to death is always awe inspiring. There are biblical models for this literary genre. God summoned Moses to die (Deut. 32:48–52). God sent the prophet Isaiah to King Hezekiah to command him to set his house in order because he would die from his illness (2 Kings 20:1). The entire plot of the medieval morality play *Everyman* is driven by the appearance of God's messenger Death to summon Everyman to Heaven and judgment. A literary scholar (Phoebe S. Spinard) has written a whole book on *The Summons of Death in Medieval and Renaissance Drama* (Ohio State University Press, 1987).

of part 2 make their preparations for death in imitation of what Christiana has done. The main action consists of last words spoken by the departing to those who remain. In turn, two subjects make up the bulk of these farewell statements—a backward glance at the person's life and future-looking statements about entering Heaven.

> Some thirty years before Bunyan published part 2 of *Pilgrim's Progress*, an Anglican preacher named Jeremy Taylor had published a classic of Christian devotional writing entitled *The Rule and Exercises of Holy Dying* (known to posterity as *Holy Dying*). It is the climax of a whole tradition of Christian thinking and exercise on how to die well. Taylor's book is a good follow-up to finishing part 2 of *Pilgrim's Progress*.

Commentary

Several very solemn literary genres work powerfully in this concluding chapter. One is the archetype of the summons to death, as the universal condition of leaving this life is made concrete and vivid by literary means. Of course the summons results in preparations for death. Another literary tradition at work is that of the farewell discourse, or more simply dying words, spoken by a person just before death (the "famous last words" genre). A parallel religious tradition is called holy dying and consists of models of people who undergo their final living moments well and in a manner to be emulated.

> A related literary genre and real-life phenomenon is the tradition of "famous last words"—the very last statements uttered by people as they are dying. Collections of such statements are readily available (including from the Internet). For the most part, such famous last words are foils (contrasts) to the spiritually charged statements uttered by the pilgrims who speak at the end of *Pilgrim's Progress*.

There is a sense in which part 2 is like part 1 in giving us a surprise ending. We are given no account of Christiana's reception into the Celestial City. In fact, we do not even see her cross the river. But there is another sense in which the collection of leave takings by various pilgrims seems entirely logical and satisfying. The focus of part 2 has been very communal. The pilgrimage has not been that of one person but of a traveling group. It is no surprise that we see the final moments of the pilgrims we have gotten to know as part 2 has unfolded.

For Reflection or Discussion

The subject of literature is universal human experience; the experience held before us in this chapter is facing and undergoing death. The first lesson to be gleaned from the chapter consists of contemplating what it will be like to face death ourselves. Then we can allow Bunyan's fictional characters and their farewell words to serve as prompts to our understanding of what it means to die well.

Further Resources

Virtually any edition of the text will serve a reader well. Some editions have more biblical references than others. The following two editions have critical apparatus (introductions at the beginning and notes at the end) by editors of known Christian sympathies: N. H. Keeble, ed., *John Bunyan: The Pilgrim's Progress*, Oxford World's Classics; Roger Pooley, ed., *John Bunyan: The Pilgrim's Progress from This World, to That Which Is to Come*, Penguin Books.

The following secondary sources are listed in bibliographic format.

Batson, E. Beatrice. *John Bunyan: Allegory and Imagination*. London: Croom Helm, 1984.

Dunan-Page, Anne, ed. *The Cambridge Companion to Bunyan*. Cambridge, UK: Cambridge University Press, 2010.

Frye, Roland Mushat. *God, Man, and Satan: Patterns of Christian Thought and Life in Paradise Lost, Pilgrim's Progress, and the Great Theologians*. Princeton, NJ: Princeton University Press, 1960.

Kaufmann, U. Milo. *The Pilgrim's Progress and Traditions in Puritan Meditation*. New Haven, CT: Yale University Press, 1966.

Newey, Vincent, ed. *The Pilgrim's Progress: Critical and Historical Views*. Totowa, NJ: Barnes and Noble, 1980.

Ryken, Leland, James C. Wilhoit, and Tremper Longman, eds. *Dictionary of Biblical Imagery*. Downers Grove, IL: InterVarsity, 1998.

Sadler, Lynn Veach. *John Bunyan*. Boston: Twayne, 1979.

Whyte, Alexander. *Bunyan Characters*. Eugene, OR: Wipf and Stock, 2000.

Glossary of Literary Terms Used in This Book

Adventure story. An action-packed story of spectacular events, often (but not always) involving the fantastic.

Allusion. A reference to past history or literature.

Archetype. A plot motif (e.g., the quest), character type (e.g., the villain), or image or setting (e.g., darkness) that recurs throughout literature and life.

Character/characterization. The persons and other agents who perform the actions in a story.

Fantasy. Literature that includes characters, settings, and events that do not exist in the real world.

Foil. Anything in a story (e.g., a character, plotline, or setting) that sets off something in the main story by being either a parallel or a contrast.

Genre. Literary type or kind, such as story or poem.

Hero story. A story that narrates the exploits of a central character who is largely (but not necessarily wholly) exemplary and whose experience is representative of people generally and the culture of the author specifically.

Narrator. The internal presence of a storyteller within a story.

Pastoral. Literature that portrays rural settings and rural living; a form of nature writing; such literature exalts simple living.

Plot. The carefully organized sequence of actions and events that make up a story, arranged as one or more conflicts that reach resolution.

Realism. Lifelikeness; literary presentation of characters, events, and settings that really happen in our world.

Romance. Stories that include elements that are supernatural or marvelous instead of strictly realistic or lifelike.

Satire. A work of literature that exposes vice or folly.

Setting. The places where events in a story occur; can be temporal as well as physical.

Symbol/symbolism. A thing, person, or action that represents something in addition to itself; based on the principle of second meanings.

Symbolic reality. A situation in which there is such a preponderance of symbols in a text that a reader chiefly encounters a forest of symbols rather than literal things.

Travel story. A story built around a hero's journey to a succession of places.

Type scene. A set of common ingredients that recur in a given type of story or event within a story and become an expected part of such a story.

ENCOUNTER THE CLASSICS
WITH A LITERARY EXPERT

HAWTHORNE'S
THE SCARLET LETTER

HOMER'S
THE ODYSSEY

MILTON'S
PARADISE LOST

SHAKESPEARE'S
MACBETH

Enjoy history's greatest literature with the aid of popular professor and author Leland Ryken as he answers your questions and explains the text.